What rea‹

"What a fun story…"　　　—Robert Johnston

"A delightful (and educational) read!"

—Alicia Hugg

"Every day is an adventure for the Lockwoods. You can taste the food, feel the breeze, suck up the atmosphere, and laugh with them as they glide through the Atlantic ocean waves."　　　　　　　—Patti Wilson

"A great read.…"　　　　　　—Joseph I.

"As a senior, I would recommend this book for anyone thinking of traveling by cruise ship or just wanting to dream about cruising."

—Amazon customer

"A real, palpable, hopeful love story …."

—Amazon customer

CRUISING
THE
ATLANTIC

A TRAVEL MEMOIR

Al & Sunny Lockwood

Front Porch Publishing
Mountain Home, North Carolina

Printed in the United States of America

Published by Front Porch Publishing
Mountain Home, North Carolina

Cover design by Parker Wallman
www.wallmandesign.com

Book layout by A.D. Reed
www.myowneditor.com

Library of Congress Cataloging-in-Publication Data
Lockwood, Al & Sunny

Library of Congress Control Number: 2017940058

ISBN-13: 9781942016328
ISBN-10: 1942016328
Travel

First Print Edition April 2017

Travel memoirs by Al & Sunny Lockwood

Cruising the Mediterranean

Finding Ourselves in Venice, Florence, Rome &
Barcelona

Cruising the Atlantic

Cruising Panama's Canal

"The great thing about getting older is that you don't lose all the other ages you've been."

—Madeleine L'Engle

CONTENTS

INTRODUCTION

When Norwegian Cruise Line's ship Epic first sailed in 2010, it was the third-largest cruise ship in the world. Its 19 decks could accommodate more than 4,000 passengers and a crew of more than 1,500.

Norwegian Cruise Line ships sport hulls painted with bold, bright and colorful artwork by such artists as Peter Max, Guy Harvey and David "Lebo" Le Batard.

The Epic's hull art was created by the company's internal marketing team. The design—rolling waves of aqua, red and purple—is meant to convey the sleek and modern amenities passengers enjoy on board.

Amenities like a rock climbing wall, a water park with yellow and purple twisting flumes, two bowling alleys, 20 dining venues in addition to 20 bars and lounges set the Epic apart from more traditional cruise ships.

Epic's ice bar and squash court were the first for any cruise line. And the ship boasts three separate children's and teen activities areas.

In 2014, the only larger cruise ships were two from Royal Caribbean: Oasis of the Seas and Quantum of the Seas.

The Epic is 1,081 feet long. That's longer than three football fields laid end to end. It is 133 feet wide. Its gross registered tonnage: 155,873.

It is definitely a mega cruise ship.

Although we have cruised on Holland America ships, Celebrity ships, and Princess ships, the Epic would be our first megaship.

WHO WE ARE

The first time I saw Al Lockwood he was reading one of his short stories at a weekend writers' retreat in the Gold Rush village of Volcano, California.

He stood trim and tall before 40-some retreat attendees, looking even taller in his cowboy boots and white Stetson. His story was about young men in Navy uniforms desperate to stay alive in the stifling and dangerous jungles of Viet Nam.

As he read from the pages he held in his large hands, his story made us laugh and weep, and when he finished, we all applauded. Al Lockwood had a way with words.

Later in the day, I saw two women poets talking with him. He was nodding, tilting his head to catch their words. And then, all three of them burst out laughing. The scene charmed me ... a man listening intently to women (instead of talking to them) and being fully entertained by them.

By chance, at the Saturday night banquet, he and I were seated at the same table. That's when I learned he was a photographer specializing in wildflowers of the mid-Sierra.

I had recently left an administrative post in the Communications Department of U.C. Berkeley and had moved to Calaveras County, a Mother Lode county on the western slope of the Sierra Nevada Mountains. With two business partners, I'd bought a monthly community newspaper and was attending this writers' retreat to network and, hopefully, find writers for our paper.

What I found was a talented wildflower photographer who loved the Sierra as much as I did, who had a fun sense of humor, and who was interested in becoming photo editor of our newspaper.

Following the retreat, Al and I worked together

and enjoyed the process.

Our friendship grew beyond the newspaper endeavor. He took me on photo shoots, introducing me to wildflowers with improbable names like pussy paws, fairy lanterns, farewell-to-spring.

I included him in neighborhood dinners. He shared some of his poetry with me. I shared a few of my short stories with him.

We learned that our backgrounds differ dramatically. He was an only child of a West Coast family and spent his earliest years on his grandparents' farm. I was the first of three children in a Midwest *Leave it to Beaver*-style family bustling with uncles and aunts and cousins.

Still, Al and I share several interests in common. We both graduated from San José State University, he with a double engineering degree: electrical/mechanical; I have a degree in writing. We both hold more than one graduate degree.

We care about and nurture our spiritual natures.

We both had early marriages that ended in divorce. And neither of us has children.

Although we both love music, we don't love the same kind. He favors twangy "geetars" and I prefer silky strings. I also love 20th-century popular music, especially from the 1950s when Frank Sinatra and Julius La Rosa were singing (or perhaps establishing) the Great American Song Book.

We both love to read. Like music, our reading tastes differ. I'm primarily a non-fiction fan. He devours thrillers. Yet we both also enjoy other kinds of literature. Our favorite stores are bookstores.

We've established a tradition of reading aloud to one another before going to sleep each night. That way we have something interesting to talk about at breakfast.

So far, we've read fiction (*The Number 1 Ladies Detective Agency* series), nonfiction (*Undaunted Courage* by Stephen Ambrose and *Midnight in the Garden of Good and Evil* by John Berendt), children's books (Laura Ingalls Wilder's Little House series), biographies and poetry. At last count, we'd read 70 books together. And there are many more we want to share.

We both love art. We enjoy exploring galleries and visiting artist studios.

And we both love to travel. Whether it's just a day's drive to a nearby spot we've never seen before or a lengthy journey to a different part of the globe, we share the curiosity that fuels wanderlust.

What's around the bend? On the other side of the hill? In that forest? What do people in that town like to eat?

In the beginning of our marriage, we wandered around with a tent and sleeping bags. But the passage of years and the unwelcome arrival of medical issues changed that travel style.

We bought a camping trailer and pulled it up and down the West Coast, visiting Death Valley, Yosemite, Monterey, Mendocino and other beautiful places.

Speaking of the passage of years, isn't it shocking how quickly we cross the threshold from middle-age to "old." When we're kids, a year is an eternity. We wait forever for Christmas or our birthday to arrive. But somewhere around the age of 50 time shifts into fast-forward mode and there's no catching up as the weeks and months and years flash past.

One day you're 45 and the next day you're 65 and wondering where the years went. At least that's how it seems to me.

I think the natural response to reaching "old age" is total shock. Followed, almost immediately, by the fear that the fun times, the good times are at an end.

Allow me to reassure you.

Al and I met when I was in my 50s and he was

nearly 60. Now I'm nearly 70 and he's heading for 80. As the years pile up, our energy decreases. Naps offer more frequent and welcome breaks. Instead of a long hike up and down a woodland trail, we're more likely to choose a game of Scrabble.

Yet, despite arthritic knees, heart disease and diminished hearing, our days are full and our dreams are rich and our travel adventures continue.

AL THINKS WE'RE A PERFECT EXAMPLE OF OPPOSITES ATTRACT

Contrary to popular opinion, there are advantages to getting older, foremost of which (at least in my experience) is the way that old legitimizes forgetfulness. So it is that as I think back to when Sunny and I first met, my mind is a tabula rasa: a blank slate. What else do you expect of someone my age? It's not my fault that I don't remember.

But something caught my eye back then, for I was most definitely not in the marriage market. But in less than a year we were exchanging rings and pledging our troth.

That something would surely have included two unique qualities. First, Sunny's ability to capture the flow of a story. I love a good story-teller. And, second, her effervescence.

I'm the kind of guy who sees the glass as nearly empty, soon to be dry—and the water wasn't that good anyway.

Sunny sees the glass as nearly full and "Oh Boy, isn't that wonderful! Let's rejoice and be glad!" Her effervescence was/is captivating. I've never seen anything like it, then or now. It brightens my days.

It's been her enthusiastic style throughout our 16 years of marriage.

I consider us the poster children for Opposites Attract. That I would say so is itself an example of opposites attracting. She is always pointing out how much we share in common, while I can't help but notice how very different we are.

We have different tastes in matters of music, politics, religion, foods, daily schedules and more.

Of course, none of that matters to the heart, which is the only place that anything matters.

What else can this old, unsentimental male say of my beloved? Everything I've written here seems to describe the family Labrador Retriever. You know: trustworthy, loyal, helpful, friendly.... Trouble is, it's a fairly accurate description of the woman I love.

HOW WE STARTED CRUISING

In 2012, a serious car wreck convinced us to pursue our dreams.

On that fateful Sunday evening in July while we waited at a red light, a texting driver slammed full-speed into us, totaling her car and ours and ruining our summer. Although no bones were broken, we were pretty bruised and battered. Our summer filled up with doctor appointments, wrangling with insurance companies and shopping for a replacement car.

That frightening wreck made us dramatically aware of how fragile and precious life is. How it can be snatched away in the blink of an eye, even when you're doing nothing more risky than sitting at a red light.

That's when we decided to start doing things we'd talked about and thought about doing "someday." And most of those things we'd dreamed of were travels.

First on Al's bucket list was a cruise through the Panama Canal. One of the greatest engineering feats of the 20th century, the Canal had long sung a siren song to my engineer husband. I discovered, while on that cruise, that the ship was filled with wives like me whose retired engineer husbands had dreamed all their lives of sailing the most famous shortcut in the world.

Al and I had such a grand time on that cruise that we wrote a book about it: *Cruising Panama's Canal: Savoring 5,000 Nautical Miles and 500,000 Decadent Calories.*

Our 264-page travel memoir was a finalist in the 2014 National Indie Excellence Awards. More than 100 enthusiastic readers have left reviews of our book at Amazon.com. Among them, top Amazon reviewer William D. Curnutt said this: "Their writing is inviting, funny, contagious and just flat out a joy to read."

Donna Peck, editor of *Celebration Traveler* magazine, said, "These are definitely people I want to hang out with. The repartée between husband and wife keeps the pace lively and engaging."

After the Panama Canal, we registered for a Mediterranean cruise. I love Venice, and we found an affordable cruise that began and ended in that romantic Italian city of shimmering canals and sleek gondolas.

The book that came out of that trip, *Cruising the Mediterranean,* was named Best Non-Fiction Book in the 2016 Seven Sisters Book Awards competition. And it won the Gold Medal for Adult Non-Fiction in the 2016 Wishing Shelf Book Awards, which are chosen by reading groups. (All the books in our category were read by a reading group in London and another in Stockholm.)

We're thrilled with these awards from organized review groups, but we also love hearing from everyday readers who like our books. And even from those who don't like them: we've tried to learn from those readers how to write an even better travel memoir.

We've learned that fall or spring cruises are less pricey than cruises booked at peak summer vacation times. Because we're retired, we can easily take a trip during the "shoulder seasons" (April through mid-June or mid-September through October). And so we registered ourselves for the dream-come-true cruise.

However, our creative attempts to avoid jet lag going over to Europe, and avoid flying altogether coming back, morphed our 12-day Mediterranean cruise into 42 wondrous days of exploration. Thank goodness we're retired. I doubt we could ever have taken such a long trip back in our gainfully employed days.

Here's how the expansion took place. We added four days to the beginning of our trip and flew to Amsterdam. The original goal of those four days was to get us through jet lag before we climbed aboard the cruise ship. I did not want to start my bucket-list journey foggy from jet lag.

Amsterdam turned out to be one of the best parts of our trip. A truly fascinating city. Like Venice, it's filled with picturesque canals and charming bridges.

Then as I began imagining what it would be like to end my dream cruise by climbing on a cramped and crowded airplane and roaring through the skies for 10 hours to get back to San Francisco, I realized I couldn't bear such an ending.

For me, flying is the pits. Ever since the airlines reduced seat size, stopped serving warm meals, started charging for baggage, and in general turning a flight into a nightmare, I've disliked flying.

I can't always escape the airlines, but I always try.

So I searched online and found a repositioning cruise. Fourteen easy days at sea, sleeping in the same bed every night, enjoying gourmet meals and fun entertainment, for about the price of one coach seat airplane ticket from Venice to San Francisco.

And I snatched us a reservation just like that.

Then we discovered that we had twelve days between the end of the Mediterranean cruise and the start of the cruise home. Twelve days, which I immediately began filling up with plans.

We'd spend a day in Venice after our cruise and then catch the train to Florence and explore that art-drenched city. Then take the train to Rome and visit the Colosseum, the Sistine Chapel, and little out-of-the-way neighborhoods, getting to know a few local secrets of the Eternal City.

Then a short flight to Barcelona and a week learning about Antoni Gaudi and his amazing architecture. Al would explore the bakeries of Sarria in all their chocolate wonder, and we'd just have ourselves a blast until we could board Norwegian Cruise Line's Epic and head for home.

We saw so much and did so much and learned so much that if we wrote a book about the trip it would be too big to hold in your lap. So we've written three easy-to-hold travel memoirs.

The first, *Cruising the Mediterranean*, covers our visit to Amsterdam and our 12-day cruise, which took in Venice, Athens, Istanbul and some beautiful Greek isles including the most beautiful of all, Santorini.

The second memoir of our trip, *Finding Ourselves in Venice, Florence, Rome & Barcelona*, is about our 12-day exploration of these world-famous cities.

And our third travel memoir is the one you are reading now: *Cruising the Atlantic: Our Epic Journey from Barcelona to Miami*. This book is all about our trip home on the third-largest cruise ship in the world. Here you'll read the good, the not so great and the disappointing aspects of the ship and our experience.

But I must warn you, few things upset me enough to make a big deal over them. I don't know why, but I'm almost always pleased with life — especially when I'm on a trip, seeing new places, eating new foods, and meeting new friends.

In the old days, cruise passengers filled out paper forms near the end of the cruise where they could rate the ship, the meals, the service, etc. Today, we do it all online.

But in those earlier days, there'd be scores of us in the library or buffet area, filling out our forms. And I remember more than one person saying something like, "What night was that that the steak was cold?" because they were registering a complaint on their form.

And I'd think to myself, "What? The cruise wasn't perfect for you? Someone else made your bed every day, cooked all your gourmet meals and favorite snacks, transported you to fabulous cities and you're grousing about one disappointing entrée? Especially when you're free to return it to the kitchen and order something else.

"You didn't lift a finger to take care of yourself all cruise long, and you're whining about one cold meal?"

But that's just me. That's how I think. So you won't see any deeply anguished observations from me in this book. Nonetheless, we'll do our best to be honest about our experiences.

And I must add (in case you are wondering), that we take these journeys on our own, paying for them from our modest travel funds. No cruise line or other travel organization sponsors us.

Who are we? You can consider us one of those couples who met and married late in life and have found the arrangement more than satisfactory.

We write our books to share the fun, and to encourage other older folks to fulfill their own travel dreams. If we can take such trips, despite our age, health issues and limited retirement income, you can too. Your dream trip might be to visit a national park, take a train trip across the country, or a fishing weekend in the mountains. Or it may be a cruise.

Whatever you've longed to do, we encourage you to take the first step: research and plan your trip. Research and planning are   almost as fun as going. Once you decide what you can afford, go for it. We've found travel relaxing, refreshing, renewing. And I suspect you will too.

WHY WE LOVE CRUISING

Al and I enjoy road trips and weekend getaways. But ocean cruising has become our favorite long-distance form of travel. Here's why:

Value. The price of a cruise includes transportation, lodging, all the meals and snacks we desire, entertainment ranging from movies to Broadway-style musicals and other live performances as well as a rich array of onboard and off-ship activities.

Depending on our room choice, we can be as thrifty or extravagant as we wish. Inside rooms are the least expensive. They are smaller and have no windows, which might be a problem if you suffer from claustrophobia. But I like them not only because they save us money, but also because their inside coziness and no-window darkness make for great sleeping.

The cost increases for ocean view rooms and rooms with private balconies. Suites are the most expensive, but offer the most amenities. If you are in the splurging mood you can even reserve suites that include butler service.

Convenience. We unpack once. Someone else does all the "driving." We never have to check a map or double-check a GPS. We're just along for a lovely ride.

Comfort. Cruise lines aim to pamper. No matter the cost of a stateroom—from suites to inside cabins—we'll find luxurious bedding, fluffy towels and wash cloths and very nice soaps and shampoos. Some lines include body lotions, cotton balls and (on your pillow each evening) a little foil-wrapped chocolate.

Social life. Cruising offers opportunities to meet others who share our interests. Sharing travel experiences can form the basis of lifelong friendships.

Togetherness. There's nothing like carefree travel together to renew or deepen romance. Cruising is the travel style for making great memories without a lot of stress.

Ease for aching bones and joints. At our age, with limited mobility and diminishing energy, knowing our cabin is nearby is most reassuring. If our knees give out or our energy lags, we can simply go to our cabin (our little home at sea) and take a nap. Or we can ease into a chair in the library and read a book. Or we can find a deck lounge and watch the sea go by.

We don't have to climb stairs, since cruise ships have elevators. If our knees or hips give out completely we can most likely rent a scooter or wheelchair and continue to get around onboard.

Medical help nearby. The cruise ship has a doctor on board. We find that reassuring. However, medical care is not included in the cost of the cruise. Should you need medical attention, you will be charged for it.

Destinations. Cruises take us places we're unlikely to visit on our own. This transatlantic cruise makes only three port stops on its watery journey from Barcelona to Miami, but they're interesting stops: Funchal, Madeira (Portugal); Philipsburg, Sint Maarten in the Caribbean, and St. Thomas, also in the Caribbean. Although we didn't choose this cruise for its ports-of-call destinations, these are places I've never seen before. I look forward to exploring them.

IMPORTANT CRUISE CAVEAT

Each cruise line has its own personality, and each cruise is unique. We try to describe the cruise we chose in enough detail that (if you've never cruised) you can gain an accurate idea of the experience in general, as well as a more intimate glimpse of this particular cruise.

If our easy-going style of travel doesn't appeal to you, believe me, you can find many cruises jam-packed with lively events. To be truthful, this Epic cruise offers more than enough activities for even the most energetic of passengers.

Aside from traditional cruises, many lines offer theme cruises, holiday cruises and other cruises with special-interest activities.

I encourage you to do some online research to discover exactly what cruise line and what itinerary most appeals to you.

You might find such research fun. I always do.

Cruising the Atlantic: Our Epic Journey from Barcelona to Miami

Cruising the Atlantic

.

FIRST RULE OF TOGETHER TRAVEL: MAKE TRAVEL DECISIONS TOGETHER

How could I have known that solving a travel problem would seriously upset my Sweetheart?

It was the spring of 2014 and we were planning a long dreamed-of trip to Europe. We'd made reservations with an Airbnb host in Amsterdam, and were registered for an autumn 12-day Mediterranean cruise that would start and end in Venice.

But I'd worried about the trip back home to California after our cruise. I don't like to fly and I can't stand long flights. The planes are crowded, the seats uncomfortable. If that's not bad enough, I usually get stuck by someone who's coughing or sneezing through the entire trip. Somehow, roaring through the sky at several hundred miles an hour seems so inhumane.

Almost every day at breakfast I'd mention

my concerns and Al would glance up from the newspaper and express sympathy.

One morning I announced that I'd thought of a solution.

"I'm going to do some research and see if I can find a repositioning cruise to get us back from Europe," I said. He nodded assent and went back to the newspaper.

As you may know, repositioning cruises are among the most affordable cruises available. A repositioning cruise takes place when cruise lines move their ships from one area (such as the Mediterranean during the summer season) to another (such as the Caribbean during the winter season). Since our European trip would take place in October, I thought we might have a good chance of finding a repositioning cruise to bring us back home to the states.

And I found exactly what I was looking for: a 14-day cruise from Barcelona to Miami.

The best part was that the cruise price (for the two of us) was about the same as the cost of one coach seat ticket to fly from Venice to San Francisco. I couldn't believe the fabulous price.

Fourteen easy days of beautiful sunsets and delicious food, a comfortable bed each night, and live entertainment instead of 10 miserable hours in a cramped and crowded plane.

While I wasn't sure how far Barcelona is from Venice, I knew that everything in Europe is fairly compact. And the price was unbelievable!

I called immediately and signed us up, gleefully paying the $400 deposit. The remaining $612 would be charged to our credit card in a couple of months.

I spent about 10 minutes dancing around the house, delighted with my find. Couldn't wait to tell Al what a great deal I got for us.

Later, while shopping in the produce section of our local grocery store, I began to wonder how much time we had between the end of our Mediterranean cruise and the beginning of this transatlantic cruise.

Why hadn't I checked before reserving our room? What if the Epic was leaving Barcelona before we could even get off our Mediterranean cruise in Venice?

Standing in the checkout line with my broccoli and lettuce, other questions arose. What would our options be if time was tight? Was there a train from

Venice to Barcelona?

As soon as I got home, I did what I should have done in the beginning, I checked on the date and time for boarding the Epic. And I was relieved to discover that the timeline between leaving our Mediterranean cruise and boarding our transatlantic cruise was not tight. Not tight at all. In fact, we'd have 12 days between ending our Mediterranean cruise and starting our cruise home from Barcelona.

Twelve unscheduled days. Again I cheered and danced. We could plan a whole 12-day exploration of cities I love—Venice, Florence and Rome—and we could spend several days in Barcelona, a city neither of us had ever been in.

I just knew my Sweetheart would be thrilled with the money we'd be saving, the pleasure of a restful cruise back home and the extra days we'd have to enjoy some of the world's great cities.

The minute Al walked in the door, I told him of my wonderful, affordable find.

He wrapped me in his big, warm hug and said, "Congratulations!" Then, "What's the ship like?"

I didn't know. All I knew was that we got a great deal on the price. We wouldn't have to fly back from Europe. We'd have extra days to explore wonderful cities and these added benefits wouldn't break the bank.

After supper, I went to my office to write my weekly newspaper column. At the time, I wrote a weekly feature column for *The Union Democrat* newspaper based in Sonora, California. Since our European trip would take us away for six weeks, I had to get six extra columns finished and filed before our departure.

As I worked, I heard Al say, "Oh no!" and a few minutes later, "Oh no!"

I walked to his desk to see what was causing such distress. He looked up from his computer screen, face sagging with surprise and sadness. "The Epic is a mega-ship," he said.

"So?" I asked.

"Who wants to cruise on a mega-ship? There's going to be thousands and thousands of people on it. Crowds everywhere. I can just imagine the lines."

While it is true that we've never cruised on a mega-ship, and neither of us wants to be smothered by throngs of passengers in bathing suits and flip-flops, I just couldn't share his spirit of disappointment. We're saving money and not flying home on a cramped and disgusting airplane.

"Well, honey, let's just wait and see," I said and returned to my office.

Soon I heard, "Oh, no! This is the pits!"

I went back to Al. "What now?"

"I'm reading Yelp reviews of the ship," he said, not looking up from his computer screen. "And there are lots of negative reviews. Did you know the inside state rooms are tiny?"

All inside staterooms are tiny, I thought to myself. And pleasantly affordable!

"And the bathroom is all split up, with the toilet and shower separate. And the sink is actually beside the bed. And worst of all, they have see-through walls. So if you're on the john, you're visible."

I hugged Al and kissed his forehead. "Sweetheart, I promise not to watch if you're on the john."

"I'm just saying this is not good news."

Now I think it's important to point out that Al and I have virtually never argued over anything when it comes to the many trips we've taken. But I could feel an argument coming.

"I wish you had done a little research," Al said. "These reviews are terrible. Who wants a postage stamp room with a see-through toilet?"

I took a deep breath, feeling slightly guilty for failing to check the Epic reservation with him before signing us up, and said, "It might not be a bad as you think."

Shaking his head regrettably, he said, "I don't have a good feeling about this."

"Look, we're saving money. We're also saving wear and tear on our bodies. Passing through time zones on a slow-moving cruise ship is a lot easier on us than slamming through them in a jet."

He just stared at me.

"And," I said, hoping to reassure him a little, "if our experience turns out to be horrible, we'll write about it. People love to read about other people's misery."

He gave me a "Yeah, sure" kind of look and we both returned to our computers.

As we counted down the days to our European trip, Al found more and more negative online reviews about the Epic cruise ship. He read that there were kids running wild everywhere on board, and crowds so thick that you had to wait for tables in the main dining room. He read that cigarette smoke from the casino permeated the entire ship. He read that the food was bland.

And so we started on our European dream vacation with a sort of underlying dread about how our trip would end.

WANDERING THROUGH WONDERS

From the moment we arrived in Amsterdam in late September, all during our 12-day Mediterranean cruise, and as we rambled through Italy's famous cities, we more or less forgot about the Epic.

Our days filled up with exploring the world like kids again.

As John Steinbeck once said, "People don't take trips—trips take people."

That's one of the wonders of travel, isn't it—going somewhere unfamiliar and being totally swept away by the experience.

In Amsterdam, we stayed in a 17th-century home in the Red Light District. We cruised the historic canal ring, spent most of a day in the Van Gogh Museum, photographed swans floating in serene neighborhood canals and visited the tallest windmill in the city.

In Venice we saw all the famous sights and still had time to wander through neighborhood squares with laundry hanging out to dry, photograph picturesque doors and windows and gondolas, and feel beauty saturating our hearts.

In Florence we met Father Alexander, who has been serving Mass in the Duomo for more than 40 years. We stood at the feet of Michelangelo's sculptural masterpiece: David. We walked the city, strolled along the Arno River and over the medieval stone bridge, Ponte Vecchio, to the Pitti Palace.

In Rome we stayed in an Airbnb apartment, enjoying a truly non-tourist neighborhood with mom and pop restaurants, tiny grocery stores, and lots of friendly neighbors.

Our apartment was right around the corner from the Colosseum. Yet we seemed miles away from tourist crowds.

We spent a day at the Vatican, stood awe-struck in the Sistine Chapel and were stunned by the size of St. Peter's Cathedral.

And, in general, we were bedazzled by the

history and aura and energy of the Eternal City.

And for the last five days we've been sampling the fullness of life in Barcelona. Bakeries filled with tantalizing cakes and cookies. Sagrada Familia's humongous spires reaching for heaven. Antoni Gaudi's curvy, whimsical architecture in Park Guell. And the crowded Ramblas stretching from city center to the Columbus monument at the harbor.

Today—Sunday, Oct. 26, 2014—we say farewell to this amazing Catalonian city and head for home on board the Epic.

Our 128-square-foot cabin is both cozy and affordable.

OCT. 26 - HEADING HOME

Our last morning in Barcelona is gentle and quiet.

For the past five days, the street just outside our cozy Airbnb apartment has roared with traffic. Cars, trucks and taxis rushing past in a flash, purposefully heading somewhere.

The taxis here remind me of big bumble bees. They're shiny black with brilliant yellow doors. And they're always buzzing by.

But this morning as I open the floor-to-ceiling windows in our living room, the street is serenely empty. Catalonian flags of independence hang from apartment balconies all along the street. The flags have four red stripes on a bright yellow background. And at one end is a blue triangle holding a big white star.

The citizens here in Catalonia want independence from Spain. These colorful flags are one expression of that desire.

All week long, they've flapped in the wind, but this morning they drape peacefully over balcony railings, hanging straight and still in the early morning light.

As the sun brightens the sky overhead, a few people stroll the sidewalks with small dogs on leashes.

Fresh morning air wafts through our apartment as we pack up and prepare to depart.

Because our home for this past week has been a comfy little Airbnb apartment, we must clean up after ourselves before we leave. I wash our breakfast dishes while Al sweeps the premises. Our housekeeping doesn't take long.

Al packed all his film, photo equipment and electronic gear last night. This morning, after broom duties, he stuffs the few clothes he's had out into his wheeled suitcase. I notice that he packs his film and electronic gear with much more care than his clothes.

When he finishes, he checks email on our iPad.

"Good news," he says.

I turn toward him to hear what it is.

"The Giants won last night. Eleven to four."

"Hooray!" I shout. The San Francisco Giants are

playing in the World Series, and it's been impossible to watch the games or get any information about them. Since our iPad is Wi-Fi rather than Internet-connected, we have been limited in our coverage of the Series. We've had to wait until one of our Bay Area friends sends an email telling us what's going on.

I love the Giants and want them to win the series. If we were in California, we'd be watching every game. But here in Europe, baseball holds no interest. So there's no TV coverage. I've been out-of-touch with the team I love. Now I know that the series is tied 2 to 2. How I hope they win.

Maybe we'll be able to catch a game or two on the ship.

Embarkation starts at 11 a.m. today, so we say good bye our apartment at 10:30 a.m. Although our street seems empty, a taxi pulls right up as we reach the curb with our bags. Each of us has a wheeled suitcase and a backpack. The taxi driver knows exactly where the Norwegian Epic is moored (at Terminal A), and before we know it, we're at the dock.

The Epic is not the only ship in the harbor, but it is by far the largest. And the crowds gathered in its area are huge. People, people everywhere, in couples, family or friend groupings, or standing dazed and solitary.

Almost as soon as our cab pulls away, a youthful woman in a Norwegian uniform approaches us with a smile. "I'll take your bags," she says. We watch as she puts a room tag on each one and sets them on a wheeled cart. We keep our backpacks.

A uniformed young man points us to a waiting area inside a warehouse-sized building. Row upon row of plastic chairs fill the mammoth space, most of them holding people and their carry-ons, but we easily find two seats for ourselves. Everyone in this area is speaking English—some with accents that sound Canadian or British.

While embarkation and disembarkation are often the most complicated and unpleasant aspects of a cruise (Al calls it "the military tradition of stand around and wait"), I always feel the excitement of anticipation rise before boarding.

What will the ship be like? What will we see on our journey? Will I find great books in the library? What will the evening shows be like?

Although there are always lots of activities on board, one of the things I like best about cruising is all the unscheduled time. I love having nothing to do. Long hours of emptiness to fill however I please make me feel young and carefree.

The wife of the couple sitting across from us says they're from Florida and have just spent 30 days in France. I wonder what it would be like to spend 30 days in France. I have great memories of visiting Paris and Grenoble and Annecy decades ago when I was tooling around Europe just for the fun of it. Thirty days would allow a person ample time to explore more deeply into the countryside. By the end of 30 days you could almost feel as though the place was your own.

Now this couple is headed home to the States. They inform us that last night was a time change and we all gained an hour.

That means Al and I have arrived here an hour before the ship will begin boarding. In view of all the other people who are milling about, I'm glad we came early.

Soon a uniformed man directs us to the registration desk. Travelers from the States and Canada register at one desk. All others register at another desk.

Our registration desk is a lengthy counter, with several stations for check in. When Al and I step to the counter, a woman who looks about our age examines our passports. Then she takes our photos (think driver's license photo) and says our boarding number is three.

She also gives us our room key. The credit card-sized plastic room key will double as our charge card while on board. And it will be our check-out, check-in pass should we leave the ship at a port of call.

I say to the woman, "It looks like you're really busy today."

She nods. "We're checking in 3,500 guests between noon and 4 p.m."

I guess a lot of people like us don't relish flying across the ocean, preferring to enjoy 14 days of pampering as they glide in a more civilized manner from Europe to the States.

Soon we hear the announcement that all passengers with the number three can go aboard. And off we go.

We leave the huge building, walk a short distance and enter a large elevator. When we step off the elevator, we're directed across a bridge and onto the ship.

Balloons of yellow, pink, blue, green, red and lavender line our path. And uniformed crew, standing side-by-side, greet us with smiles and a cheery "Welcome aboard."

I love the colorful and enthusiastic hospitality.

"That was pretty painless," Al says. "How long did we wait? Half an hour, 45 minutes?"

Our first desire is to find our room (#10041). It doesn't take long, even though hundreds of others are searching for their rooms, too. Everyone is polite, and the elevators fill and empty easily.

Our Deck 10 stateroom is on a long, long hallway. We soon learn that all the hallways are long on the Epic.

Here's a tip on cabin choice if you think you might be prone to sea sickness. An inside cabin seems to feel less movement than an outside cabin. And a cabin near the center of the ship feels even less movement. Cabins on higher decks feel more movement than cabins on lower decks.

Not that there's much movement with these huge floating resorts to begin with. Aside from size, cruise ships have stabilizers built into their structure that help reduce rolling and bobbing.

Still, for sensitive folks, a centrally located inside cabin is the best for minimizing the possibility of sea sickness.

I rarely experience sea sickness and Al never does. Nonetheless, we feel good about reserving a central inside cabin for this cruise.

And we're happy when we find our cabin, slide our room key, and open the door. Stepping inside with our backpacks, we see just how small our room is: about 128 square feet. The queen size bed is straight ahead, with slight space on either side for a bedside table. The place is clean and neat.

The closet seems huge, large enough to almost step inside. Its curving walls and interior lights make it a perfect place to stash our backpacks. There are plenty of hangers and a safe for our valuables. Complimentary robes and slippers await our use.

Across from the closet, are a makeup table with three large drawers, a big medicine cabinet and cubbies holding towels and wash clothes. We have a fridge, ice bucket and hair drier. And, pleasantly, a dirty clothes hamper fits neatly under the counter connected to the makeup table.

On the table, a bottle of champagne and a plate of chocolate covered strawberries greet us. What a surprise! Who could have sent us this treat?

Just then we hear a knock on our door. It's our housekeeping steward, Christine, and her supervisor, Angel. They introduce themselves and welcome us, saying if we need anything just let them know.

I ask if the TV has a sports channel.

"Channel 24," Christine says.

Now I'm excited. I might get to watch a World Series baseball game with my favorite team.

After our brief chat with Christine and Angel, we decide to taste-test the chocolate covered strawberries. They're excellent. But who left them for us?

Then we try out the bed. It's comfortable. Al points out a pleasant surprise—goose-neck reading lamps, one on each side of the bed.

These adjustable LED lights are plenty bright for reading, yet don't fill the room with light, so one of us can sleep comfortably while the other reads (or in my case, writes). How cool is that.

Unfortunately, the bathroom is just as Al described it. The shower, in its opaque stall, is on one side of the entry door. The toilet, in its opaque stall, is on the other side of the entry door. This could be quite embarrassing if someone knocked on the door while we were using either of the facilities.

The sink is on a counter connected with the

makeup table.

But Sweetheart does not make a big deal out of the bathroom arrangement.

I notice a blinking light on our telephone console. We have a message from a man named Louis, a guest services crew member who says he's available to us for any need.

His recorded message says, "I've reserved space for you at the Manhattan Dining Room for 5:30 p.m. We hope you enjoy cruising with us."

When I tell Al about the welcome phone call, he says, "Wow! How nice is that."

We celebrate the welcoming phone call by eating another chocolate covered strawberry apiece, savoring the combination of tartness and sweetness.

Then, it's time to find an open dining room for lunch.

The Garden Cafe, with seating for 728, is on Deck 15. We ride an elevator up five decks.

Lots of other passengers have the same idea, and as we approach the hallway leading to the Garden Cafe, the crowd thickens. I hear a woman's voice loudly welcoming diners, and when we reach the entry, the buffet-style restaurant spreads out before us. It is huge. And it is beautiful.

White lattice and flowery decor make the place actually feel like a garden.

Located over the bow, the Garden Cafe stretches from one side of the ship to the other. All the serving stations are located in the middle. As we wander by, checking out the various offerings, servers in tall white chef hats await our requests. There are made-to-order pasta stations, Asian food stations, made-to- order omelet stations, traditional American fare stations and so much more.

Al settles on roast beef, mashed potatoes and green beans. I tease him about the originality of his choice.

I fill my plate with steamed green beans, roasted eggplant and sweet peppers and other delicious veggies. Everything is fresh, colorful and tasty.

And for dessert, we share a slice of German chocolate cake.

There isn't a bad seat in the place. The eating area is only four tables deep. Every table has a great floor-to-ceiling view of the sea. It's a beautiful arrangement.

After weeks in Europe, we find ourselves eating at a slower pace, and lingering over dessert. It feels good to be at our final destination ... the floating resort where we'll live for the next 14 days.

After lunch, Al returns to our cabin and I go on a get-acquainted tour of the ship.

Most of the public rooms—restaurants, shops, entertainment venues—are on decks five, six and seven. The group tour begins on Deck 7. We visit lounges and an array of shops where passengers can buy clothes, perfumes, jewelry and trinkets of all kinds.

Our tour guide shows us a room where folks gather to play bridge.

Someone in our growing tour crowd asks where the library is, and the guide looks abashed. "We don't have much of a library on this ship," he says, pointing to a tall bookcase with glass doors across the corridor from the Sand Bar Lounge.

Since the ship library is one of my favorite places, I make my way to the bookcase and check out its contents. The books are few. And none of them is in English.

"Where are the English books?" I ask the guide.

He says more books will be delivered tomorrow. But today the crew is busy getting passengers on board and settled.

This is not a propitious introduction to the Epic's

library. Fourteen days at sea and only one bookcase of books? And none in English? But I'll check back tomorrow.

Our group descends to Deck 6 where the casino and the main dining room—The Manhattan—are located.

The Manhattan is the largest dining room on board, with seating for 592. It is decorated in an Art Deco style. The two-story windows looking aft offer excellent views of the ocean and sky.

I think it is interesting that the Manhattan Dining Room is at the back of the ship, with huge windows looking out on where we've been as we sail. And the Garden Cafe is at the bow of the ship, showing us clearly where we're heading.

The casino sits smack in the middle of Deck 6. And it is huge—13,000 square feet. Since we are still docked in Barcelona, the 347 slots as well as blackjack and poker tables stand silent and abandoned. The casino only comes to life when the ship is at sea and in international waters.

This is one of the few public places on board where smoking is allowed and, because there are no walls enclosing the area, I can see why there would be complaints about the smoke trailing off to other parts of the ship.

Deck 5 turns out to be what I'd call the main deck. Here, the various guest service desks are located.

The atrium area has its own cafe and a three-story video screen surrounded by scores of plush, comfortable chairs. I wonder if movies are shown here.

Still on Deck 5, the guide leads us through the art gallery and photo gallery.

Other cruise lines generally schedule formal nights. During formal nights, passengers are encouraged to really dress up — men wear tuxes and women wear gowns and beautiful jewelry. During those formal nights, couples often go to the photo gallery and have their portraits taken.

Since Norwegian Cruise Lines boasts the only freestyle ocean cruising, meaning no formal nights, no set times for dining, and so on, I'm wondering when people would want to have their portraits taken. But obviously they do, because here's a photo gallery, with various sets for backgrounds.

The guide says we're now going all the way to Deck 15 and we'll hike to the back of the ship to see the pools, water slides, the spa area and other things. I decide to skip the rest of the tour. Al and I can go see those places on our own.

I turn back toward our room. When I get there, I find all but one of the chocolate covered strawberries are gone. "What happened to the goodies?" I ask.

He just grins, looking up from his iPad where he's stashed his reading library.

I tell him about the pathetic on-board library. His response: "You should have brought your Kindle."

At 3:30 everyone is required to take their orange life jackets out of the closet and go to an assigned place for the ship emergency drill. Al and I are assigned to gather in the Bliss Lounge on Deck 7.

Off we go with our life jackets in tow for our briefing on emergency protocol. I always appreciate these drills. They take place before the ship launches, and they make me feel safe. If there's any problem during our cruise, we'll all know what to do and how to do it.

Sweetheart and I reach the lounge fairly quickly and wait while all the others arrive. Eventually, everyone is accounted for and the demonstration begins. We learn how to put on our life jacket. How to fasten it. And how to unfasten it. We learn what to do and where to go if there is an emergency. Emergencies are announced by a series of emergency

27

alarm tones: seven short tones and one long.

Unlike airplane safety briefings, where passengers ignore the demonstration, on the Epic every person is required to attend the emergency drill. We're told if anyone skips the drill they'll be escorted off the ship.

When the drill is finished, we make our way back to our cabins. Because of the crowds, it's slow going.

But when we finally get "home," our suitcases are waiting for us.

For the first time in almost two weeks Al and I have the pleasure of actually unpacking everything and moving into our new little abode. We find pleasure in shaking out shirts, blouses and sweaters from cramped suitcases, and slipping them on hangers where they can once again hang free and easy. We unfold our slacks and hang them. We set our toiletries in a cubby above the sink. I note that in addition to shampoo, shower gel and hair conditioner in the shower, the Epic also supplies us with nice bottles of body lotion.

By the time we get everything organized and our suitcases placed beneath the bed, it's time to start thinking about dinner.

Although the Epic does not expect people to dress formally for dinner, we don't want to look like we just tramped in from the field. So I slip on some dressy slacks and a matching top and Al changes his jeans for a nice pair of black trousers. He adds a collared shirt and silver tie, and we're off.

Our Deck 10 cabin is midship, and the Manhattan Dining Room is aft on Deck 6. We take the nearest elevator down four decks and as we walk the long, long, long corridor, we're reminded that the Epic stretches out farther than three football fields laid end to end.

We pass the Headliners Comedy Club, O'Sheehan's Neighborhood Bar & Grill (with its two-lane bowling alley), and walk through the casino.

And as we leave the casino, a young man in a crisp white officer's uniform approaches us. "Welcome, Mr. and Mrs. Lockwood." He extends his hand. "I am Louis."

I recognize his voice from the welcome message on our phone.

Al and I are astounded. "You know who we are?" I ask.

"Yes. Yes," he says smiling. "Did you enjoy your

champagne and strawberries?"

"Were they from you?" Al asks.

"They're from all of us on the ship," he says.

"We loved the strawberries," I say. "Thank you so much. Is this the kind of welcome everyone gets?"

He laughs. "We know you write travel books."

And suddenly I understand.

I explain to Louis that we don't drink alcohol but would love to exchange the champagne for a bottle of sparkling apple juice. He says the change will be made before we return to our room.

Then he walks with us to the Manhattan Dining Room and introduces us to the hostess there, a beautiful young woman at the welcome desk. "Take good care of them," he says to her. Then, turning to us, he hands each of us his business card. "Remember, if you need anything, just call me."

We thank him for his attention and promise to call if we want anything.

The hostess speaks to a waiter who leads us through the large restaurant all the way to the back, and seats us at a table for two next to a huge window. We are the only people in this part of the restaurant. I love the quiet ambience, the secluded location, and the sunshine pouring through the window.

We can sit here and gaze out at the sea and sky, or look the other way and see the entire dining room. Soon its tables will be filled with families and friends enjoying gourmet fare while waiters gracefully carry huge trays piled high with dinners and drinks.

I'm glad we're here early, so we can enjoy a gentle intro to the evening rush.

A waiter removes our wine glasses and fills our water glasses. The menus he hands us present many choices, including vegetarian dishes and low-calorie fare.

Al selects French onion soup for his appetizer, grilled shrimp with broccoli and rice for his main dish. I order crab cakes with slaw for my appetizer and, for my entrée, green curried chicken with rice and grilled vegetables.

Ours is a spacious table for two. Not far from us is a small stage for an evening dance band. And in front of the stage, a lovely dance floor.

Soon our appetizers arrive and we begin our dinner.

As we eat, the restaurant fills with other diners. They come in pairs and groups and families. Not an unhappy face in the crowd as they take their places around tables large and small. We're all just beginning our trip across the Atlantic and it's clear everyone's looking forward to the adventure.

When our entrées arrive, the ship pulls away from the pier and Al says, "We're standing out to sea."

"Yes," I say. "Good bye, beautiful Barcelona. You have given us so many wonderful memories."

While we enjoy our meal, the maître d' stops by our table to introduce herself: Violeta Bratu.

The three of us engage in friendly small talk. When she asks if we expect to eat dinner in the Manhattan each night, we assure her that that's our plan.

"And will you be wanting it at about this time? About 5:30 p.m. each evening?" she asks.

I laugh because we've just spent weeks in Italy and Barcelona where everyone starts eating supper at 8 or 9 p.m. We, who are hungry by 5 or 5:30, always felt out of place.

"Yes," I say. "We'd love to eat at 5:30 each evening."

"Well," she says. "Then I will reserve this table for you for the entire cruise."

Al's face is alight. "That's wonderful," he says. "I love the view."

She smiles. "I'm happy to make this table yours." Then she's off to welcome someone else.

"I'm blown away by the friendliness and kindness of these people," Al says.

It is quite remarkable.

"I think they want us to write a book about them and say good things in it," I say.

"Can't say anything bad about this experience," he replies.

Our waiter asks if we want a dessert menu.

You bet we do.

Al orders cherry cheesecake. I have pistachio crème brûlée. And our waiter brings us each a cup of decaf coffee.

We linger as night gathers outside. I love sunsets and sunrises at sea. With this dinner table, we'll be able to enjoy the sunset every evening.

When we finally leave and make our way through the restaurant, the place is full and there's quite a line of people at the welcome desk waiting for tables. Thank goodness we eat early.

Although a number of shows are available tonight—Legends in Concert, Howl at the Moon, and Cirque Dreams & Dinner—we skip the entertainment. It's been a full day and it feels good to settle into our sweet little home at sea.

We open our bottle of chilled apple juice, pour ourselves a glass and toast love. And the joys of travel.

By 9 p.m. we've both showered and changed into our pajamas. As Al takes his nighttime pills, he glances at me with a twinkle in his eye and says, "Aren't we the last of the big time partiers."

Oct. 26 - Heading Home

We love the fresh and colorful salads available with lunch or dinner.

OCT. 27 - FIRST DAY AT SEA

The Garden Cafe is nearly empty at 7:30 a.m. when we stroll in for breakfast.

Morning sun shines through the windows, lavishly filling the restaurant with light, warming the beige carpet and cream-colored table tops.

We each take a tray and wander from station to station trying to decide on what we're hungry for while the ocean sparkles enthusiastically just beyond the windows. Our first full day at sea and it's going to be a beauty.

Our table is one of many awaiting breakfast diners. Al digs into his French toast slathered with strawberries. On another plate is his small serving of scrambled eggs. He also has orange juice and coffee.

I have Muesli and coffee. The coffee is disappointing. About that we agree.

Tomorrow we'll go to the Deck 5 restaurant,

Taste, for breakfast and see if its coffee is any better.

"Life's too short for insipid coffee," Al always says.

While the Garden Cafe is a help-yourself buffet affair, passengers are not expected to bus their own tables. Several gold-jacketed crew members keep the tables clear and clean.

After breakfast, back in our cabin (and it's a long walk to our cabin), we study our *Freestyle Daily* newsletter to see what we might want to do today.

At home, we'd read the daily newspaper. But here, basically free of world crisis cares, we check out the daily newsletter.

Freestyle Daily, an 8-1/2-inch by 11-inch publication, is delivered every night, left in the mailbox right beside our door. It contains a detailed schedule of the day's activities—everything from group Sudoku in the atrium to blackjack tournaments in the casino to lectures, classes and meetings. It also contains ads for the daily specialty drinks and descriptions of the evening's various entertainment offerings.

I see that the fitness center, with its treadmills and cross trainers, is open from 6 a.m. to 11 p.m. Plenty of time for anyone who wants a workout.

I should go there and get in the workout routine. Maybe tomorrow.

It looks like a group gathers each day at 9:30 a.m. on Deck 7 to walk a mile together on the outdoor jogging/walking track. That's something else I should probably do. But not today.

We read that the ship will be passing by the Rock of Gibraltar between 9 and 11 a.m. Now there's something we want to see.

Last night I checked the sports channel on the TV, hoping to catch a World Series game, but no such luck. Only soccer was being broadcast. Sigh.

SHORE EXCURSIONS

Al picked up a shore excursion sales sheet at the main desk and he's now checking out what's available during our port of call stops.

Shore excursions are land tours. All cruises offer them. Non-cruise companies also offer tours at the various ports where passenger ships dock. Sometimes we buy a shore excursion. Often we simply sightsee on our own. On past cruises we have also teamed up with another couple or two and hired our own guide for the afternoon or evening.

Depending on the port, shore excursions offer

active tours such as ziplining, biking or perhaps taking in a live concert, and less active sightseeing tours. Sightseeing tours are typically bus tours that drive to the highlights of the area including museums, cathedrals or famous neighborhoods.

There are half-day tours, full-day tours, and sometimes evening tours. In Barcelona, we bought a dinner cruise on the Bosporus Strait as a shore excursion.

Shore excursion prices can vary from about $40 per person to hundreds of dollars. Buying a tour in every port can add hundreds or thousands of dollars to your cruising bill.

Knowing what you want to see and do at a port stop can help determine whether you buy a tour or simply explore on your own. We often take our camera and note pad and just wander the nearby area. On our own we can spend as much or as little time as we wish at a cafe or a beautiful park. We can browse interesting shops, take our time photographing architectural details, spend precious moments in a church or chapel, or just enjoy the carefree pleasure of walking around in an unfamiliar but fascinating place.

Such independent wandering is not advisable,

however, in third-world countries. And it's not advisable if the ship docks far from the sites of interest.

Years ago, we were on a cruise that stopped in Cartagena, Colombia. There were sites we wanted to see and I thought we could hire a taxi at the pier to take us into town where we could just wander around on our own.

At the time, we were cruising on a Holland America ship. I went to the tour coordinator to ask about our plan. She discouraged me.

Our ship would dock in an industrial area to refuel and take on supplies. "It's a long way from town and the area between our ship and Old Town is dangerous," she told me.

I asked her, "How about just hiring a taxi to take us to Old Town?"

"You could do that," she said. "But if you hire a taxi, I urge you to lock the doors and roll up the window the minute you climb inside."

That warning and other information she imparted convinced me to open our wallet a little wider and spring for a short walking tour that would take us to the main sites we wanted to see in Old Town.

Looking back on that experience, we made a wise decision. Except for aggressive sidewalk salesmen, the tour was a good one. Our guide answered most of our questions and kept us entertained with humorous stories. The group was made up of older people (like us), so the pace was comfortable. And we came home with great photos of Old Town architecture, artwork, streets and squares.

When it comes to shopping for ports of call tours, you can go online before your cruise to see what excursions your ship will make available.

On line, you can also see what alternative tours may be available at each port. And you can check out reviews of various tours at cruisecritic.com.

Or you can wait until you are onboard to do your shopping.

This transatlantic crossing has only three stops along our way. We are scheduled for a stop Wednesday at the Portuguese island of Madeira. And later on we'll be stopping at Sint Maarten and St. Thomas in the Caribbean. Our cruise will end in Miami.

Al and I try to be careful shoppers when it comes to shore excursions. We've learned that such organized tours are often overpriced. At the same time, if we shop wisely, we may get some real value for our dollar.

On a cruise-sponsored tour, the boat will wait for passengers should they be late. There's no such guarantee for those who wander on their own, or who line up a local tour with an independent guide.

Glancing up from the tour list he's been studying, Al says the prices are quite reasonable and he thinks we should sign up for the "Scenic Village and Coastal Views" tour available at Funchal on Madeira. It's $50 each for the afternoon tour. Sounds good to me. So we go to the shore excursion desk to register for the tour. But it's too early. The desk is not yet open. We'll have to come back later.

Then it's off to the Garden Cafe where we plan to sit at a table and watch as we pass the Rock of Gibraltar.

It's nearly 9 a.m. when we reach the restaurant, wander through, and find a seat at the very bow of the ship. The place is filled with people eating breakfast. Their trays hold plates of eggs, breakfast meats, pancakes and waffles, or bowls of hot cereals. There are also sticky buns, breakfast muffins, croissants (plain and chocolate) as well as sliced melons and a breakfast berry mix of blueberries, strawberries and raspberries.

We hear lively conversations in German as well as English. Obviously, we're not the only ones eager to witness the famous limestone rock rising 1,398 feet off the southwestern tip of Europe. Everyone, it seems, has come to eat and watch.

The Rock of Gibraltar commands the entrance to the Mediterranean and has been a British territory since 1713.

A drawing of the dramatic rock has served as the logo for Prudential Financial since the early 20th century. In 1969 John Lennon and Yoko Ono were married at the British Consulate at Gibraltar. How cool is that!

All of us gathered here are eager to see this powerful landmark.

But, alas, it is not to be. As the Epic glides along on the morning's calm sea, thick mists form a curtain that completely hides the Iberian Peninsula's most famous landmark.

Disappointed, Sweetheart and I decide to visit the pools and water park up on Deck 15.

When we step out of the elevator and turn toward the pools and fountains, we find the crowds Al has dreaded. Throngs are swimming and splashing around in the pools, or sitting on the edge, laughing and kicking the water.

Or they're stretched out on lounges, soaking up the sun.

The Aqua Park has two pools and five hot tubs and people pack them all. Everyone's having a ball. If we ever need a little energy boost, this is the deck to get it.

Beyond the pools, the outside decks sport rows upon rows of deep blue sun lounges, all filled with folks in bathing suits.

What grabs my attention are the multi-storied water slides. Twisting tubes of purple and yellow and green far above us carry eager sliders, squealing and screaming with joy. On The Epic Plunge, riders drop 200 feet into a pool, much to their delight.

Everywhere, people are happy and having fun. And that makes me feel happy, too.

We wander through the Aqua Park Kid's pool area with its shallow splashing pools and funky statues of friendly gators and pink starfish.

A poolside cafe has breakfast fare, and a Waves Pool Bar serves colorful drinks.

As we wander, we discover a quieter, less crowded area over near the giant chess board. Here the deck is open and we can enjoy the sky and ocean. We grab a couple of chairs and just watch the sea go by for a while.

It pleases us that on this huge floating resort filled to the brim with passengers, we can find someplace quiet to read or simply dream as we watch the ever-changing sea.

AL'S MUSING ON OUR INSIDE ROOM

I'm a film photographer. No, I don't make movies; I photograph with a camera that uses film. You know, that plastic stuff that comes in rolls that your ancestors used to use to take pictures. Yes, the small black and white photos you have stored in an old shoe box under the bed or in the attic.

Because I work with film, I have a darkroom where I process my film and make prints. It's much like a medieval alchemist's laboratory. Cramped, dark, and often smelly. I love it. I guess that's part of the reason I prefer inside cabins when we take a cruise. They're sort of like being back home in the lab, but nicer.

The main reason we choose inside cabins, though, is that they're the lowest-priced accommodations on the ship. All we do in our cabin is sleep and shower, anyway. If we have a compulsion to see whatever body of water we're traveling in, all we have to do is go someplace else onboard and look. The buffet line is such a place, ideally next to the dessert cabinet.

Although all inside cabins are small and windowless, not all inside cabins are created equal. Floor plans vary. The amount of storage differs. Sometimes the shower's a phone booth, and sometimes rather spacious.

Thus it was when Sunny booked passage on the Epic that I immediately began investigating our accommodations. Would we find a modicum of comfort in our waterborne residence?

At first glance online, the Epic's inside cabins looked lovely. Nice bedding; clean, modern decor. Although smaller than many at 128 square feet (less than my darkroom), it looked like it'd do nicely. And then I began reading reviews.

It would appear that the Epic's designers in some burst of creative spontaneity decided that everyone else's rectangular bedroom/rectangular bath was ... passé.

So the Epic's designers put the entry passage down the middle of the room, placing the toilet—the W.C. for you Brits—on one side and the shower on the other. Both ... I need a word here ... modules are encompassed with wavy glass walls. Frosted glass.

Using either facility is a bit like getting a full body scan from the TSA: you can't quite see everything, but it's not for the bashful.

Needless to say, the reviews and comments from older travelers—who prefer a bit of privacy while performing certain bodily functions—were not exactly favorable.

There being no place for a sink in either module, the wash basin is on the dressing table at the foot of the bed. This provides excellent opportunity to watch your partner conduct his or her daily ablutions. Many older travelers commented on this too, also with less-than-enthusiastic ratings.

Travel, though, is an adventure, or at least it should be. An opportunity to try the new and unexpected. We decided that that attitude was the way to deal with our stateroom's eccentricities, so we settled in determined to enjoy the voyage.

But (confidentially) I'll be glad to get home to my darkroom. And a bath without a see-through door.

***

At 10:30 a.m. we head to the Epic Theater for a shore excursion lecture on Funchal, Madeira, where we'll stop tomorrow.

When we reach the theater, we discover that a throng of other passengers has the same idea. The place looks full. Nonetheless, we're able to find two adjacent seats.

The presentation turns out to be refreshingly practical. While the speakers don't load us up with a lot of history or background on the town itself, they present useful information on each shore excursion being offered.

They point out if there are lots of stairs to climb, if the tour requires substantial walking and if the walking is on hillsides or uneven pavement. They tell us if the bus we'll be riding is air conditioned or not. Good, practical information to help us decide on shore excursions we might like to take.

Since Sweetheart and I are among the older passengers on board, information on stairs and walking surfaces is invaluable. With Al's arthritic knees, extensive walking, climbing or standing are experiences we must avoid. Luckily, the shore excursion we've chosen will work for us. It's a bus tour with a few stops, and we can handle that.

After the lecture, at the shore excursions desk we sign up for "The Scenic Village and Coastal Views" tour.

At noon, it's Taste for lunch. Unlike the Garden Cafe buffet, Taste is a contemporary restaurant where we sit and order from a menu. We share an order of hummus and pita chips for our appetizer. Then we each order the same meal: lettuce salad with goat cheese, poached salmon with green beans, and for desert baked peach with almonds and cream.

While we enjoy our meal, we're enveloped in beautiful and familiar melodies. The talented fingers of Juan Carmelo bring the nearby grand piano's keyboard to life as he plays "Misty," "What a Beautiful World," "Young at Heart," and other familiar songs.

A delicious lunch accompanied by lovely live music: the entire experience is exquisite.

I glance at Al. His eyes are brimming with tears.

"Are you OK?" I ask, worried that some unbearable pain is causing him grief.

He nods, unable to speak. He looks down at the table cloth for a moment, then at me.

"I'm just overwhelmed with gratitude," he whispers.

AL'S MOMENT OF GRATITUDE

There we were, having lunch in the Taste dining room. The pianist adding pleasantly familiar music to our quiet meal, when somewhere between the hummus and the salmon, my heart suddenly filled to overflowing with warmth.

I felt overcome with the awareness of how truly rich my life is, how truly blessed I am. And I teared up.

In a less public setting, I'd probably have bawled.

There is so much to be grateful for. If I were to make a list, it'd fill an encyclopedia.

In that moment, all my little grumbles just faded away. Sitting there with my beloved, sharing an excellent meal accompanied by music, and realizing the care we were receiving from ship staff ... it all coalesced in my heart. These blessings are gifts, freely given, without expectation of return.

And in that experience, I realized that our future days at sea on this huge ship filled with passengers would become days to be savored and cherished.

CIRQUE DREAMS AND DINNER

After a brief, refreshing nap, I go to the reservations desk and get our tickets for tonight's Cirque Dreams and Dinner show.

Making reservations on a cruise ship is a new experience. Past cruises, on other lines, have offered one evening performance at about 8 p.m. and the same performance (with perhaps a touch more adult content) again at 10 p.m.

But the Epic has several small theaters in addition to the large Epic Theater, each offering evening entertainment. And because there are not enough seats in the smaller theaters for everyone, tickets are required.

Most of the smaller theaters are free (included in the cost of the cruise). But the Cirque Dreams and Dinner show costs $30 a seat. I hope the show—a theatrical dining experience—is worth the ticket price.

As the young woman at the reservations desk hands me our tickets, she says, "The show starts at 8:30 but get there by 8 because it's first come, first served."

I'm grateful for the tip.

Later, as Al and I dress for dinner, we wonder what the show will be like and hope we'll be happy that we spent the extra money for it. Despite Al's dislike of arriving early, we are at the Spiegel Tent 45 minutes before the dinner and show is scheduled to begin.

The Spiegel Tent is a theater in the round, designed to look like a circus tent. There are two dining levels—main floor, where we'll be seated, and a balcony arrangement above.

We're led to a curved booth which we share with another couple—Bill and Wendy from Southern California. The four of us enjoy a short, lively conversation before the lights are dimmed for the show.

The dinner, a preset menu, is served (and eaten) in the dark, as brilliant, fantastical circus acts fill the central stage with color and nonstop action.

The show starts with a fellow balancing a wine glass on the blade of a knife he's holding in his mouth. This particular performance progresses throughout the show, until he ends up balancing a chandelier on top of an inflated balloon on the back of the knife held in his mouth.

Our roast beef and shrimp entrée is served while a contortionist does an amazing and graceful "dance" on an acrobat's swing high above us.

The array of costumes—whimsical and gorgeous—is blinding. There are wacky hats, and baggy pants, skin-tight gowns and feathery headgear. The ringmaster tries to keep control with a whip and a whistle, but, of course, the show's too big and bright and energetic and the gags are great.

The big top arena, just a hair's breadth away from the audience, fills with acrobats, jugglers, gymnasts, aerialists flying overhead, clowns and musclemen, jokesters and musicians, all in wild and colorful costumes.

Couples dance while spinning on roller skates.

There's an entire bit of magical costume changing, where one person raises a curtain around another person, then drops the curtain and the person inside wears an entirely different outfit. This happens four or five or six or 10 times. And each time, the change is instantaneous and the costume is astounding. The rapid fire costume changes ignite enthusiasm and all of us in the audience clap and shout.

There are dancers who I swear are solid muscle, dancing together on acrobat swings. Or spinning each other until I'm sure one will go flying off into the audience.

Everything is fast, colorful, and accompanied by live music.

A strolling violinist provides excellent accompaniment to the acts. Wearing a yellow and orange tux with tails, a red cummerbund and a paisley top hat, the violinist saunters among the audience and actors, providing haunting or lively or funny music. The perfect tune at the perfect time.

Dessert is chocolate petit fours and fresh strawberries. But who can take their eyes off the show to look at the food?

When the performers start searching for audience members to come be part of the act, I drop my eyes and pray that I'm not chosen.

Before I know it, a tall woman with even taller hair and eyelashes about four inches long is at our booth, tugging Bill's arm.

"Just a minute, just a minute," Bill says, as he struggles to put on his shoes.

Wendy whispers to me that Bill always takes off his shoes when he goes to the theater. She also says that he's shy.

Too late. He (with his shoes on) and other audience members are standing in the spotlight, being instructed on how to perform their part of the next act. I feel sorry for Bill. I'd hate to be him. But he seems at ease ... and the act, a humorous, somewhat suggestive western showdown, comes off beautifully with everyone laughing. Even the audience participants.

After two hours of dazzling extravaganza, the show ends.

As we four walk out together, I tell Bill how much I admire his taking part in the program. He chuckles. "When we were seated, I got a hint that I might be recruited for the show," he says. "And it was fun."

Al and I aren't ready to go back to our cabin. So we take an elevator to Deck 15 where all the pools and water slides are.

Plenty of people are sitting around the Waves Pool Bar enjoying drinks and conversation. Loud Latin music is playing in Spice H2O and dozens of couples are dancing to the beat.

Hand in hand, we stroll around the corner to where the rows of deck lounges held sunning people earlier today. Now, the place is all but empty. Nothing but vacant lounges. And a cool night wind.

At the railing we stand with the black ocean below, the black night above and the wind tossing our hair. We squeeze together to keep warm. It's fun being here without the crowd, while Latin melodies fill the background, and nothing but the sea and wind around us.

"What a show!" Al says.

And I don't think he means Cirque Dreams.

A healthy Epic meal. Fruit, grains (cake), dairy (whipped cream). Small portion for weight management. Who says you can't eat responsibly at sea?

OCT. 28 - DAY AT SEA

By 7 a.m. we're at the Garden Cafe. Again, the place is nearly empty.

"Obviously, we're on a ship of late sleepers," Al says. Then adds, "I was going to say slackers, but decided not to be so judgmental. Besides, I like having the place all to ourselves."

So do I.

I choose scrambled eggs and fruit for breakfast. And I add a fresh-baked chocolate croissant from the pastry bar.

"Coffee's good this morning," I say after my first swallow.

I brought our *Freestyle Daily* to check out today's activities.

"Look at this," I say. "This afternoon there's a language class in Portuguese. Let's go and learn a little Portuguese before we visit Madeira. Then we can say something in the local language while we're there."

Al nods.

"Oh and look, there's a class in calligraphy. Wouldn't that be fun to learn?"

That's when Al announces, "I plan to take a course today called Loafing 101."

As we continue with breakfast, I decide that after 28 days on the road and three days at sea, it's time for a haircut. My shaggy do needs a shape-up.

Back in our room, I call the salon for an appointment and am told there's an opening at 10:30. I ask how much a wash and trim costs and am told $75. That's more than twice what I pay back home, but my hair really needs refreshing so I make the appointment.

The beauty salon is on Deck 14. (I can just hear Al saying, "The moment you go from beauty 'shop' to beauty 'salon,' you raise the price of everything 30 percent.")

When I arrive, I'm asked to wait in the reception area. Here the chairs are sleek and modern. Restful music fills the background. Scented steam rises gently from a black ball about the size of a basketball in the center of the room. The steam gives the room a warm and cozy feel. Dark wood walls frame the waiting area, but the space is full of light from large windows just beyond this reception room.

A slim young woman in a chocolate-brown uniform greets me with her name: Alissia. She will be my hair dresser today. She leads me into the salon, a long room with light sea-green tinted tile walls and a row of empty chairs sitting in front of tall mirrors. Beyond the mirrors is the ocean.

The ocean side of this room is all glass. That explains the brightness of the space. I wonder if the salon is gloomy when it's storming outside.

Looks like I'm the only customer this morning. That's a surprise. I thought the place would be humming with gossipy conversations, while scissors clipped and hair flew.

Alissia is from Australia. She says she loves working with hair. I can tell she loves it by the caring way she shampoos and conditions my hair.

Her scalp massage almost puts me to sleep.

Back in her chair, she studies my hair, lifting a few strands above my ears and looking at it this way and that. Then lifting a few strands from the top and the back, she carefully considering what she will do. I say I just want a shape-up, but I don't want so much taken off that I look like I just got a haircut. She laughs.

And then she begins to cut. She combs and cuts with great care. Not much hair is falling from my head. She combs and cuts, and combs, and studies the results and cuts some more.

After adding a protein-based curl enhancer, carefully working it through my hair and picking out all my curls, she says, "I'm finished," and hands me a mirror to check it out.

It's beautiful. I love what she's done.

When I go to the desk to pay for the service, I find an 18 percent gratuity added to my bill. So my shampoo and trim costs $88. Visiting the salon is one way cruising costs can add up.

I've never before had my hair done while on a cruise. And at this price, it will be a long time before I ever have it done again. But it looks lovely and I'll be stylish for the remainder of our cruise.

Al and I take a quiet window table in Taste for lunch. We're the only couple in the restaurant. I like the serene emptiness.

We order hummus and pita chips for an appetizer. We've had it before and love it.

Just beyond our window, the sea has turned gray and the waves have grown large. The sun no longer sprinkles glitter across the waters. Its light is flat and cool. Even though I'm wearing black tights and a sweater, I feel a little chill.

Al has a BLT sandwich for lunch. I have a big veggie salad.

Right after lunch, I head for Deck 7 and the library, hoping there will be some interesting books to check out.

I find the little glass-door bookcase across from the Sand Bar Lounge. There are a few more books on its shelves than yesterday. But still the shelves are mostly bare.

I see several English titles, and quickly read their spines, or pull them off the shelf to read their titles. Most are about dogs. There are a few mysteries. A cookbook or two. But, in effect, nothing that grabs my interest.

The pathetic library is a major disappointment. On other cruises, the library has been one of my favorite places with long shelves sagging under the weight of travel books, best sellers, biographies and novels. We've been on ships with libraries of more than 1,000 books, plus magazines and board games and jigsaw puzzles. But I guess I'm out of luck on the Epic. Strange.

You'd think that a transatlantic cruise, with its

many sea days, would be the most likely to have a library filled with good books. Maybe I'll check back later in the week.

At 2:30 I'm off to the Bliss Lounge for Portuguese Language Class. This is the place Al and I went when we first boarded to learn what to do in case of an onboard emergency.

Today the place is full of people who want to learn a little Portuguese.

I have no facility for languages. Al, on the other hand, seems to easily pick up words and phrases of various languages. He can speak a little Spanish, a little German and bits and pieces of other languages. But he does not join me for the afternoon Portuguese language class. I'm hoping to learn to say "thank you" since that's probably the only useful phrase I'll need for our short visit to Madeira.

The young man leading our class gives us some background on the language. He says Portuguese is the eighth most spoken language in the world. He says it's the language of Brazil and that five million people in Africa are native Portuguese speakers. As he shares interesting information, he passes out a sheet of paper containing basic Portuguese words and phrases.

We practice counting and some of the numbers sound like Spanish. 1: um(a), 2: dois (duas), 3: tres, 4: quatro, 5: cinco, 6: seis, 7: sete, 8: oito, 9: nove, 10: dez, and so on. Al would love this. He'd be counting to 50 before I'm at 10.

The word for water is easy: "Agua."

The phrase, "Hi, how are you?" in Portuguese is: "Oi! Tudo bom?"

"Yes" is "Sim."

"No" is "Nao."

"How Much?" is "Quanto custa?"

And there are many more phrases. For each one, the teacher illustrates the pronunciation and then we all mirror him. Some words and phrases are easy. Others are not. People get to laughing at their crazy mispronunciations. But we try again and again.

The Portuguese word for "thank you" is "Obrigado." I say it over and over. Obrigado. Obrigado. It sounds almost musical. I think I can remember it. I hope to use it tomorrow.

The class lasts about an hour. It's fun and funny and everyone seems to have a good time.

When we leave, we take our sheet of words and phrases with us.

As I head for our room, I begin to feel

uncomfortable. Sort of buzzy. Sort of head-achy and stomach-achy. Could this be seasickness?

I'm not prone to seasickness. But once before, on a cruise to Mexico, I began to feel like this and was told to drink ginger ale. It did the trick within minutes. Since then, I've brought a few pieces of candied ginger with me when we cruise.

Back in our cabin, I dig out the candy and eat a piece. Soon the unpleasant feeling passes.

SEASICKNESS

Anyone who has suffered from seasickness or motion sickness knows how miserable it can be. It can be caused by a repeated rocking motion.

It is also caused when the inner ear senses that your body is moving, but your eyes don't see any movement. This conflict between the senses causes motion sickness.

I've heard that women are more prone to seasickness than men.

Symptoms include nausea, stomach cramps and headaches. While there are medications for seasickness, for me, a little ginger does the trick. It can be a can of ginger ale. A cup of ginger tea. Or chewing some sugared ginger candy.

Others have suggested green apples and dry soda crackers. In fact, green apples and dry soda crackers is one of the choices on the room service menu.

Going out on deck for fresh air and a good long look at the horizon also helps, I'm told.

***

After dinner—roast lamb for Al, lasagna for me—we head for Spice H2O where the movie *Gravity* is being shown on a large outdoor movie screen. The ship calls the evening movies at Spice H2O "movies under the stars."

Al and I loved *Gravity* when we saw it in the theater and we look forward to tonight's showing out under the stars. But, alas, it's far too cold for us. Perhaps if we'd brought a blanket or two we could have stayed. But the night wind is chill and cutting, so we go instead to Maltings (one of the many lounges on the ship) and listen to Jim Capik play his mellow guitar. A perfect ending to our day.

Later, in our cabin, we play a hard-fought game of Scrabble on our iPad, before retiring.

Madeira countryside is all cliffs and terraces.

OCT. 29 - FUNCHAL, MADEIRA

After two days at sea, viewing only miles of gray or blue waves, this morning we're sailing past the lovely island of Madeira.

Its lush green hills and white buildings are a beautiful sight. We shall dock later today at Funchal, the capital of Madeira.

The Garden Cafe is unusually crowded and bustling at this early hour. Obviously, others are also excited about today's port stop.

Al's tray includes a serving of French toast, scrambled eggs, mixed berries and sausage. I get scrambled eggs, corned beef hash, a small bowl of muesli and mixed berries. And we get coffee. Not the best, but it will do for now.

As we enjoy breakfast at our window table, we study the hilly island we'll visit this afternoon on our shore excursion. White buildings scatter down the emerald hillsides like cubes of sugar. The sun sets windows ablaze and warms the cliffs. Tall bridges span deep crevices. And some amazing cliffs plunge into the blue sea. In fact, our afternoon tour will take us to Cabo Girao, the second-highest cliff face in the world.

We're told the dramatic near-vertical drop is more than 500 meters (1,900 feet).

After finishing our breakfast, Al goes to the pastry bar and gets each of us a chocolate croissant while I refill our coffee cups. The coffee's just okay, but the croissants are wonderful.

On the way back to our room, I detour to the guest services desk to see if I can find any information about the World Series. I haven't been able to catch any games or any coverage of the games and I'm eager to know how the San Francisco Giants, the team I love, are doing.

Everyone behind the guest services desk is young and Asian. When I ask about the World Series, the man waiting on me looks puzzled. It's clear that he hasn't the slightest idea about what I'm asking.

"It's an American sport," I say. "Baseball. Can you check the Internet and see if the Series has ended?"

He types something into his computer, and I can see that he doesn't understand what is showing up on his screen. His brow wrinkles as he reads his screen. I'm dying to know what he's reading.

Very slowly he says, "There is no winner."

"What's the score?" I ask.

He studies his screen. "It is 3 to 3."

"Oh, that's wonderful," I say. "Thank you."

"No problem."

The Giants are still in the Series! Six games and the two teams are tied. Tonight everything will be decided. Oh how I wish I could watch it!

I cross my fingers, hoping my small gesture from half a world away will help the Giants win tonight and become world champs for the third time.

Rushing back to our room, I share the good news. Al seems almost as happy as I am. We hug, clap a couple high-fives, and wish we could watch the last game tonight.

Then I notice that he has the TV on.

"The movie *Apollo 13* is about to start," he says. "I've ordered room service. I'm sure we can squeeze in the movie before our afternoon shore excursion."

We both love *Apollo 13* starring Tom Hanks, so we settle in for a journey back to the 1960s space race.

***

By 1 p.m., we're in the Epic Theater, tickets in hand for our "Scenic Village and Coastal Views" tour. Everyone else on board seems to be here too. The place is packed. Enthusiasm fills the air.

Al and I are told we're part of group number 20. We'll be on bus 20. And we're each given a round sticker to wear that bears the number 20.

When group 20 is called, we file out of the theater and off the ship. Crew members check and double check our tickets to make sure we're on the correct tour.

We walk through a customs building and out to a row of large, air-conditioned tour buses. As soon as our bus is full, it pulls out of the parking lot.

A middle-aged woman is our guide. Standing at the front of our bus with her microphone, she tells us all about Madeira. Clearly she is proud of this island, her home.

She says most people born here live their whole lives on this 286-square-mile island, located 540 miles southwest of Lisbon, Portugal, and 350 miles off the coast of Morocco.

Madeira was discovered in 1418 by Portuguese sailors. They found no indigenous people or animals (except for lizards and bats) on the island. To this day, she says, there is no wildlife to speak of, no snakes nor squirrels on the island. But the city of Funchal and surrounding areas are filled with small family farms. We see lots of banana trees as our bus carries us through the town. It's as if every yard has two or three banana trees.

Our guide says Madeira exports five main products: Madeira wine, bananas, embroidery, flowers and Mediterranean fruit (including avocados).

One of the passengers asks if fishing is a big industry here since the North Atlantic surrounds the island.

The guide says, "No." Then elaborates: "The ocean is too deep here, more than two miles deep, and there are no fish close to the surface."

The man persists, asking about farming fish.

She responds with a smile. "Perhaps you saw the six circles floating off shore. They are fish containers. But it is a small fish farming operation, not a large industry. And storms often destroy the containers."

I'm glad she explained the circles, for I'd noticed them floating in the deep blue waters and wondered what they were. Now I know.

She adds, "All endeavors on this island are small.

Companies with 20 employees are considered very big companies on Madeira."

Funchal, with a population over 100,000, covers the slopes of an ancient volcano. As the bus chugs through its narrow, steep streets, our guide points out a building where Winston Churchill stayed, and describes various restaurants and hotels as we pass them.

She also describes the prevalence of banana trees.

"No one has a large number of trees," she says. "But if you have two and your neighbor has two or three, and the next neighbor has two, then all of you together can have enough fruit to export. Everyone can make a little extra money."

Even as the bus leaves the narrow, cobbled streets of Funchal and begins to climb toward Cabo Girao, we see banana orchards and gardens filled with flowers. All the steep hillsides and mountainsides are terraced and filled with vegetation—banana trees and sugar cane and other plants.

"All farming and everything else of that nature is done by hand," our guide says. "This island's steep geography prohibits the use of animals or machinery."

I can certainly believe that. I can't imagine how anyone could work these cliffsides. They're so steep, surely people would tumble down every time they tried to take a step.

"There are no mules or donkeys on this island," she says. "And only about 1,000 cows. No one can raise cattle here because of the steep cliffs."

As she continues to describe what we're seeing, the bus climbs and climbs, maneuvering through endless switch backs and hairpin turns. I begin to feel apprehensive.

When I was in my twenties, I entertained myself by jumping out of airplanes. It's true. Almost every weekend during the summer, I could be found at a small, rural airport where sky diving was the central activity.

I'd arrive early, before the daily breeze picked up, grab a chute and climb into one of the little Cessna 152s sitting beside the grass runway. And off we'd go into the wild blue yonder.

Because I was the most novice jumper, I'd be the last in and first out. Our little plane would climb to about 7,000 feet, sometimes as high as 10,000 feet. We'd make a pass over the jump zone, drop a wind indicator to see how the breeze was blowing. Then we'd circle around and fly back over the jump zone. This time, I'd climb out and stand on the (locked) wheel, while holding onto the strut under the wing.

At the proper moment, I'd let go of the strut and I'd be free falling as the plane pulled away. Within a few seconds, I'd pull the rip cord and the big parachute would open above me like a protective mushroom cap, and down I'd float in the silent morning air.

While the whole experience was exciting and scary as all get out, I loved it. Loved the thrill, the wild air rushing by as I stood on the wheel, the gentle, silent ride back down to earth. Loved it all.

But things changed after I passed 60. For some strange reason, I began to fear heights. The fear has increased as the years have passed. I don't like cable cars, don't enjoy looking over the edge of cliffs, and most certainly wouldn't climb into an airplane for the experience of jumping out of it.

So, as our bus chugs up hills that become steeper and steeper, I grow uncomfortable. In my seat next to the window, I can barely bring myself to gaze out.

The bus stops at a gift shop perched on a medium-size cliff. The bus is facing the edge of the cliff and I my stomach clenches. I can't wait to get off. Once my feet feel the earth beneath them, my stomach relaxes. The day is crystal clear and the air smells sweet.

Most of the other passengers hurry to the railing and gaze down at the fields below. I hold back. From my vantage point, I can see the carpet of terraced gardens covering the hillsides all around. It's a scene out of a beautiful painting. But I don't approach the cliff and neither does Al.

The gift shop owner has set up a table of free refreshments, including shot glasses of Madeira wine. A thoughtful way to welcome us and entice us to buy.

Almost everyone on board wants to taste the famous fortified wine this island is known for. Some passengers buy bottles to take home.

When we're back on the bus, our guide explains that Madeira's unique taste comes from the unusual practice of repeatedly heating the wine as it ages.

"This practice yields fascinating flavors," she says. And those who tasted the welcoming wine agree.

Our bus continues to climb. I ask Al to change places with me. "You should have a turn next to the window," I say. But he declines.

In 2010, he took a serious fall off our porch, breaking his back in two places. Since then, he's grown ever more apprehensive of heights.

"I guess that fall taught me that I'm breakable," he says. "And what breaks hurts. Worse than that, at this age it takes a long time to heal. And you don't always recover fully."

The bus continues chugging up and up the mountain. The views are incredible. And at the end of our long climb, we've reached Cabo Girao, the highest cliff in Europe, the second highest in the world. Our bus pulls into a small parking lot beside a shop.

In front of the shop, tables are piled high with knitted sweaters and caps, but no one stops to check out the goods or enter the shop.

Instead, the crowd from the bus heads for the cliff. Al and I follow at a distance, walking along a wide, paved path to the lookout place. Once our group reaches the edge, everyone spreads out along an iron railing and starts taking photographs.

I can't bring myself to look straight down the almost vertical drop. But I can glance out and over to see the buildings of Funchal covering the hillsides, like a chunky white blanket. The views of the ocean and the rugged hills and the terraced emerald farm fields and the winding roads take my breath away. The dramatic scenery is incredible.

Looking through the lens of my camera somehow puts enough distance between me and my fear of heights that I begin to feel comfortable gazing down.

When I get up enough courage to glance straight down for a couple of moments, I see clouds forming between us and the deep blue ocean far below. I'm so high, I'm above the clouds!

Somewhere there's a cable car and a glass-floor viewing platform, but Al and I don't go in search of either.

We take photographs until we begin to feel queasy, and then we walk back to the gift shop.

Wonderful items fill the shop. Shelves of hand-painted bowls and serving platters and dishes. Tables of embroidered pillow cases, table cloths, placemats. Stacks of knitted caps and scarves. And other hand-crafted art works from stone and wood.

As a rule, we don't buy souvenirs. Our souvenirs are our photographs. But the bright and colorful dishes in this shop instantly capture our imagination. We can't resist getting at least one platter. Sunny yellow, pumpkin orange, splashes of blue and red burst from the dish we choose. In the center stands a rooster, all plumage and crown, and around the rim of the dish, a braid of yellow and orange leads to a brilliantly red heart. Just looking at this colorful plate makes me happy.

On the back, in a lovely hand, black letters on a white background announce: "Made un Portugal. hand painted." There are numbers and other marks that I assume stand for the artist and the studio where it was produced.

We happily pay for this cheery platter. The woman at the checkout counter wraps it carefully in paper, then bubble wrap, and puts it in a protective bag. As she hands it to me, I say, "Obrigado." Her face crinkles with smile lines and I hope I didn't mispronounce my "thank you."

We ride the comfortable bus back down the mountains. I continue to occupy the window seat. As the afternoon sun casts long shadows across the terraced mountainsides, they begin to resemble an Asian painting. I've never seen views like these, and their beauty fills me with happiness.

In addition to the cliffs and gorgeous views, our afternoon tour includes a charming church and other historic buildings. We also have time to wander through parts of downtown Funchal and sit in the shade of a beautiful park.

AL DISCOVERS MADEIRA

To freely admit my ignorance, I never knew there was an island named Madeira before our ship sailed into Funchal harbor. I knew that "Madeira" was some sort of wine, made (in)famous by Flanders and Swan's song, "Have Some Madeira M'Dear," but that was it. Boy, had I missed something!

The island—it's actually an archipelago—is no less than a little jewel. Rising out of a blue sea into a blue sky like Neptune's thumb, it soars from seaside almost straight up to green mountain tops. Tiny white houses cling to those hillsides in defiance of gravity.

Every house, it seems, has a small garden. On Madeira, going out to "plow the south forty" would appear to mean weeding 40 square meters (that'd be 430 square feet), not acres. And did I mention steep? No hope for tractors on Madeira.

The loneliest man on the island has to be the John Deere salesman.

The grade must also make it really challenging to play any sport with a ball. I can just hear the children's cry. "MOM!! My ball!!"

"Never mind, son, we'll drive down to the beach and get it."

This raises the matter of driving. The island's roads are for the most part somewhat widened lizard trails, gnawed out of hillsides with the least-possible dirt removal. This didn't—doesn't—faze anyone. Our tour bus, a full-sized 30-passenger coach, swept around curves with utter nonchalance, even when the view out the window was straight down. My definition of "unperturbed" has been forever broadened.

As an engineer, I was especially intrigued by the island's aqueduct system. Because rainfall is unevenly distributed—and that's the primary water source—a whole system of aqueducts and canals has been built to provide water to homes and gardens. Some of those, I have read, are used as hiking trails.

I have to say I was really disappointed that our stay at Madeira was so short. This is a place with much to see and do. I hope we can get back, sooner than later.

***

Our window table in the Manhattan Dining Room awaits us. As we take our seats, maître d' Violeta

Bratu approaches to ask how our day went and we gush about the beauty we enjoyed. Since it's early and we're the only people in our area of the dining room, the three of us share a longer, more personal conversation.

Violeta is from Romania. She works six months on the ship and has 10 weeks off. She says she gets restless after a few weeks at home. Her parents are in their 70s and she's concerned about them. They own both a country and a city house. They prefer the one in the country, but must return to the city during the winter. She worries about them as the years take their toll on health and abilities.

I understand her concern. At our age, most of us have elderly parents. Many are sick and need care on a regular basis. These concerns come with age.

When we're young our concerns stretch out in front of us. They're all about our future: can we finish our education? Can we find a good job? Can we find a life partner? Can we help our children make their way through this complex world?

But at our age, concerns focus on our elderly parents, the deaths of family and friends and our own inevitable aging. Can we maintain our health? Have we saved enough for our retirement? Should we move to a smaller home?

While these are surely our golden years, they're also years of challenge. Sweetheart and I deal with such challenges by "living in the present." We don't put things off that we want to do. We travel as much as we can. We immerse ourselves in the creative pursuits we love—writing, photography, music. And we get out in nature.

You could say our motto is: Do it now. Because there's no guarantee you'll have another chance.

After our conversation with Violeta, a waiter takes our order.

I order one appetizer but am brought another. No problem. I eat what I'm brought.

Al's dinner is Mahi Mahi. Mine is beef stroganoff. Neither is exceptional.

Yet we love the pace of dinner here. By the time we reach dessert, the restaurant is full. And the hundreds of conversations at other tables form a comforting background babble that makes us feel at home.

We order dessert and decaf coffee. But the dessert I order is not delivered. Again I get something other than what I chose.

When I ask the waiter about the discrepancies,

he explains, "The menu is not entirely accurate. Because this is a repositioning cruise, we may not have exactly what's on the menu. So you'll get a substitute instead."

How interesting. It will be a little mystery every evening ... will I get what I order? Or will I receive a substitute?

As we linger over dessert, the ship pulls away and sets course for America. From our window, we watch the night approach. While it isn't black outside, it is that magical time of day when darkness slips across the land, and the sky is a deep blue-black. Poets call this time of day the gloaming.

As we head out to sea and Madeira grows dark, lights blink on all across the hills and valleys. Lines of white lights twinkle in the blackness, with a deep rich sky above.

This is how much of the ship looked during the day (when most people were sunning poolside). Plenty of space to make your own.

OCT. 30 - VISITING WITH EPIC'S CRUISE DIRECTOR

While getting ready for breakfast, Al combs his hair and talks to his reflection in the mirror about when he was young and the sap was still rising.

"But now," he says, turning to me, "the leaves are falling off."

All I can say in response is, "You look good to me, Mister."

And out the door we go for the long walk to the Garden Cafe.

Even though thousands of passengers are aboard this huge ship, we rarely see or hear anyone in the morning as we hike to breakfast.

At the Garden Cafe we fill our trays with good and healthy portions and enjoy another quiet breakfast as we stare at the pale blue ocean. Today's weather forecast is 72 degrees and partly cloudy, but the early sunshine is flooding in, warming and welcoming us. I love starting the day gently while the crowds are still snoring in their beds.

CRUISE DIRECTOR ARMEN PETROSSIAN

At 10 a.m. I make my way to Armen Petrossian's office. He's the Epic's Cruise Director, responsible for all onboard hospitality, entertainment and social events. And he's agreed to talk with me about his work.

With three theaters—Epic (681 seats), Headliners Comedy Club (259 seats), Spiegel Tent (217 seats)—and more than a dozen bars and lounges, the Epic presents quite a programming challenge for the cruise director.

I don't ask his age, but Armen looks like he's in his late 30s. His hair is cropped so short it could be classified as the popular bald style. He has bright brown eyes, a trim brown mustache and beard. The beard follows his jaw line, giving his face a crisp outline. And there's an energy that radiates from him.

I've seen him out and about on deck and he's always enthusiastic, always smiling.

Here in his office—a small room filled with file cabinets—I sit beside his desk.

Armen says he's loved the entertainment world since he was a teenager. In fact, as a teenager, he worked as a DJ's assistant, and later he formed his own company, Energetic Events, which provided music and entertainment for events.

So he's well acquainted with performers and what makes a great show.

A graduate of the University of Washington, he holds a degree in business administration.

"Business administration is a long way from cruise ship entertainment," I say. He laughs.

"Even when I was employed as an auditor, I was doing DJ work on the side," he explains. "I did an event for Holland America's corporate group, and they asked me to come work on the ship. So my first cruise job was with HAL."

Since Al and I have cruised on Holland America ships and this is our first time on a Norwegian ship, I ask him to compare the two lines.

"Norwegian caters to a younger crowd and to families," he says. "When I worked for Holland America, we had a two-person staff for the kids. Here we have a staff of 20 caring for kids from 3 to 17."

Then he says the length of the cruise gives him a good indication of the age of the passengers he'll be entertaining. And, of course, the age of the passengers dictates the kind of entertainment he'll hire for the cruise.

"A short cruise, say seven days or less, attracts a younger, party crowd," he says. "Cruises that last from 10 to 20 days attract more experienced cruisers, those in their fifties and sixties.

"Serious cruisers sign up for trips of 30 days or more. When I was working for Holland America, I met a woman who had accumulated 1,500 days of cruising."

The longer the cruise, the more the passengers want to learn about the ship and the staff. "They want a closer relationship with the captain and the staff, and with the musicians," he says. "They're on board longer and they just want to know more."

That's one reason he schedules "Meet our captain and senior officers" events during long cruises. These informal gatherings give passengers a chance to ask questions and even make suggestions, Armen explains. We'll have one or two such events on this cruise.

The telephone on his desk rings often while we talk. He either ignores it, or answers and says he'll call the person back. I'm pleased and impressed that he's willing to give me such undivided time.

I ask if a repositioning cruise differs in any major respect from a regular cruise. He says the difference is like night and day.

"Even the entertainment material changes," he says. "We've added a lot of dance sets. Glen Miller-type music," he says.

"The younger crowd does not dance to live music. They want a DJ. The older crowd loves live music. On this cruise we have several bands. And on this cruise we have an officer's ball. People love that.

"The under-50 group wants big parties and loud music. The over-50 cruiser has more sophisticated tastes. They want lectures. They want to learn new things. They need intellectual stimulation."

Asked what he likes best about being a cruise director, he answers without hesitation: "The chance to work with creative people. And to be creative myself. This job lets me use my right brain, my creative side. And my left brain because I'm responsible for 150 crew members who are musicians and dancers and so on."

On this repositioning cruise, there are shows featuring comedy and magic, music and dance. He says he loves working with musicians.

"They're really passionate about their job and I love that," he says.

Armen gleans entertainment ideas from TV, from other cruise lines, from the Internet and from other sources as well. "I get an idea and tweak it to fit our line and our guests. Short cruises are easier, long cruises require a lot more."

I ask him to list his standard entertainment events, those that take place on every cruise no matter the length, and he checks off several: Bingo. The Marriage Game. Salsa dance classes. Karaoke. Bowling. The list goes on.

I ask if he's added anything new for this cruise and he says "Yes."

"We've brought the caricature artist on board. He's in the atrium and our guests love having their caricature done," he says. "It's unique and specific to you. You take home a caricature of yourself."

I've seen the artist working in the Atrium and noticed that he has a long line of people waiting to have their caricature done. That sounds like something I'd like to do.

Armen talks at length about the ship's Karaoke, and about how special the passenger talent show is. "Don't miss it," he says. And I promise him I won't.

I wonder what kinds of talents the passengers have that they'd want to share in a show.

"Oh, believe me, they bring costumes and instruments," he says. "Passengers who know about onboard talent shows come prepared."

Then he recalls one of his best talent show memories. It took place on a 30-day cruise to Peru.

"We had an elderly gentleman who wanted to sing 'My Way,' for the show," he says. "This man was frail and you could tell he wasn't in the best of health. We were concerned about his performing. I mean, what if something happens while he's on stage? He had been a musician in his younger years. And he brought his trumpet on board and signed up for the talent show.

"Well, when he came out on stage for his performance, you could just feel the worry rippling through the audience. He played a few notes, and then started to sing. This little, frail guy had a really big voice. And he sang with such passion that people in the audience were standing and applauding before he was even finished."

Armen shakes his head at the memory. "Believe me, he was totally unforgettable."

As our visit draws to an end, he says, "This job

is a lot more beneficial than being an auditor. This job leaves our guests feeling happier about life. And that's a good thing."

When I leave his office and stroll back to our cabin, I think of all the work, all the research, all the thought, all the organization and management it takes to make a cruise the wonderful experience we passengers crave. And how fortunate Armen is to have found a career that's both fulfilling and fun.

***

Sweetheart and I go to lunch in the Garden Cafe. I get spaghetti and he gets a grilled chicken sandwich.

The place is a zoo. Not an empty table anywhere, so we share a table with a couple from Manchester, England. And the four of us visit while we enjoy our ice cream and cookie dessert.

Turns out this is their first cruise.

"I've dreamed of cruising all my life," the wife says. "And this trip is very disappointing."

I ask what's disappointed her.

"The air conditioning in our room doesn't work well," she says. "The TV offers nothing. There's no library. The entertainment is rotten."

I ask what shows they've gone to.

"Blue Man and Legends," she says. "Very loud rock. We don't like rock."

I can understand that. I'm not much of a rock fan either.

"What have you enjoyed?" I ask. Al gives me the elbow. He says I always go into reporter mode, asking questions people might not want to answer. But his elbow got to me too late.

The wife's face brightens. "We love the food," she says. "It all tastes great. I love the variety and the quality."

Al and I say we've enjoyed much of the food ourselves.

I ask, "Where are you headed after you get to the states?"

"Disney World in Orlando," her husband says. "Disney World is another life-long dream of ours."

Then Al asks a question of his own: what do they think about this morning's medical drama.

I don't know what he's talking about and neither does the couple from Manchester.

He says he heard the captain make the announcement over the ship's PA system.

"Well, it seems a passenger had a heart attack

about two this morning and it was a serious attack. She was in a life-and-death situation," Al says. "The captain actually stopped the ship so a helicopter could come and get the lady and transfer her to a hospital back on land.

"The captain wanted to assure passengers who had paid for shore excursions for our Caribbean stops, that he'll make up the lost time so no one will lose those excursions."

The conversation immediately turns to health concerns. One reason Al and I like cruising is that a doctor along with other medical personnel are on board. And if the health problem is serious—a life-and-death situation—helicopters can transfer us back to land.

However, on a transatlantic cruise, the ship may be out of helicopter range. Then we'd be in trouble. Thank goodness, this particular passenger had her heart attack while we were still close to Europe.

When I was young, I couldn't understand why old people were always talking about their health problems. But now that I'm in the "old people" category, I understand completely.

We talk about our health problems because we're

so surprised we have them. We don't feel old enough to be worrying about heart attacks and strokes and arthritis and all the other ills that seem to plague us now. But here we are, with "old people's problems" cropping up in our daily lives.

We talk about our health issues to find solutions for these conditions complicating our lives. (What works for your insomnia? Or your aching knees? Or your failing eye sight?) And if we can't find solutions, maybe we can at least find an understanding, sympathetic ear.

On our way back to the room, I detour to the guest relations desk to see if I can get some information about the World Series.

When I reach the Atrium area, I'm surprised to find no line at the guest relations desk. Usually a dozen people or more are waiting to get their questions answered. Eagerly, I approach one of the young men behind the counter. He looks like he might be from Bali. He beams as he asks, "How can I help you?"

"I'm trying to find out the latest on the World Series." I can see immediately that he doesn't know what I'm talking about.

"It's an important baseball game," I explain. "If

you could search on your computer who won last night's game. Just type in American Baseball World Series and tell me who won. Please."

I watch as he busily types. Then wait. I can see him reading.

"What's the news?" I ask eagerly.

"The World Series is over," he says, eyes still on his computer screen.

I am about to burst with curiosity.

"The World Series ended last night," he says. And then he slowly reads the words: "The San Francisco Giants beat the Kansas City Royals to win the series."

"Yahoo!" I shout, unable to contain my joy. He jumps, startled at my outburst.

I can't help myself. "Oh, thank you!" I say. If there hadn't been a counter between us, I'd have given him a big hug and a kiss. "You just made today the best day ever!" I hurry back to the room to share the good news with Al.

How I wish I could have seen one of the games that the Giants won. But I'm thrilled to know that our favorite team, our "hometown" team from San Francisco won this year's World Series!

Their third World Series victory!

At 2 p.m. I answer a knock at the door and find a crew member bearing a plate of chocolate-covered strawberries.

"Enjoy!" she hands it to me, turns and walks away.

"Look at this!" I show the plate to Al. "I'll bet this came from the guest desk." I pop one of the goodies into my mouth. "Someone noticed how happy I was and sent us this. Is this sweet, or what!"

We both devour the delicious treats in celebration of the World Series win.

After a few minutes, Al says, "Baseball season is over. And it ended in the best possible way. Gone are the mid-season doldrums when the Dodgers were surging and the Giants sank to the dregs and Timmy went back to the minors.

"Kind of makes you believe in resurrection, doesn't it."

Later, we take our iPad and go to the Garden Cafe for a game or two of Scrabble. Since it's well after lunch time and before supper, the place is nearly empty.

A few other passengers have claimed tables where they read their Kindles or Nooks or visit over coffee.

We take a table beside the windows. The great

Atlantic stretches out calmly in all directions rippling lazily in deep blue.

When I first met Al, I didn't know how to play Scrabble. I made only three- and four-letter words—cat, hat, met, the, red—words like that. But he taught me how to see more possibilities. He taught me to save the letter "s" so I could hook onto an existing word, making it a plural, and spell a new word starting or ending with "s." That way I'd accumulate a lot more points.

And he taught me other tricks.

Now I play Scrabble with a competitive spirit that delights in long words and creative words—whether I spell them or Al does. The game is a lot more fun now.

As we play, my points stack up. My computer-generated hands are a nice mix of vowels and consonants, enabling me to create a number of high-point words.

Al, who hasn't had such great hands, comments on my growing lead, "I've nurtured an asp to my breast."

Later in the game, feeling slightly bad because I'm more than fifty points ahead, I ask, "Would you like me to go get you something sweet?"

He looks up, eyes twinkling, "I have something sweet sitting across the table from me."

Is it any wonder that I love playing games with him?

***

Statistics for this repositioning cruise:
* The average passenger age is 59
* The youngest passenger onboard is 1
* The oldest passenger onboard is 93
* Passengers represent 54 nationalities
* Crew members represent 67 nationalities

The top five passenger nationalities are:
USA – 1,324 passengers
UK – 907 passengers
Germany – 436 passengers
Canada – 381 passengers
Sweden – 137 passengers

One segment of the hall leading to our room.

OCT. 31 - HALLOWEEN AT SEA

The ship is rocking and rolling so energetically it wakes me up. In a minute or two, Al turns over.

"She's really bouncing along," he says.

"I don't think I can go back to sleep," I say. "What time is it?"

He turns on his bedside lamp, checks his watch, and announces, "six o'clock." Then adds, "Too early."

He turns the light off and we lie in the dark as the ship groans in response to the push of wind and waves. But we can't return to sleep, so after a while we turn the light back on and rise for the day.

Off to breakfast in the Garden Cafe. Sitting with our eggs and coffee, we watch the vast dark ocean rise and fall. Its water forms ever-shifting mountains and valleys. Huge waves bear foamy crests. A vicious wind blows the foam off in ghostly sheets of white.

"This is some weather," Al says.

The dark Atlantic is almost charcoal blue. But as

the sun rises, it changes to a lighter gray blue and the sky grows bright with huge white clouds. Still, the wind and waves do not let up their pounding fury.

Al and I have taken five other cruises, yet we've never had a ride like this. Of course, we've never cruised across the Atlantic Ocean. And it's a big ocean.

AL MUSING ON THE BIG ATLANTIC

An old Breton fisherman's prayer begins, "O God, thy sea is so great, my boat is so small." I'd heard that for years, but it truly never sank in until the Epic set sail (figuratively speaking) from Madeira to the Caribbean.

Our transatlantic route spans 4,875 kilometers, or, for the metric-challenged, 3,029 miles. A distance equal to the span of the continental United States. Mere hours in an airplane. In a car, four days if you drive until you're cross-eyed. On a ship, at a blazing 20 knots (23 mph), that's—arithmetic alert—3,029 miles divided by 23 MPH divided by 24 hours per day equals ... 5-1/2 days, plus or minus.

But that's just a number.

The scale of the voyage truly sets in with the passage of time. Day One. View at breakfast: the ocean. View at lunch: the ocean. View at supper:

the ocean. Day two. View at breakfast: the ocean. View at lunch: the ocean. View at supper: the ocean. Day three: repeat. Day four: repeat. Etc.

It's not that we are bored onboard. There is more than enough to do and plenty to eat. Especially desserts, but that's another story. The daily calendar is packed with activities for those who are so inclined.

Yet there is also good opportunity to slow down and reflect. I cannot help but think that in a time when everything's interconnected; when the blueberries in our California grocery come from Argentina; when if-it's-Friday-it-must-be-Madrid, the greatness of our precious blue planet has become somewhat diminished. A long voyage is a good— perhaps necessary—reminder of that diminishment. We've lost something vital in our daily rush.

As Sunny and I make our way across the Atlantic, I realize that the Breton fisherman had it right. And, remember that he was in a tiny trawler filled with smelly fish, bobbing like a cork in bad weather. I'll take the Epic. Everything (and everyone) smells better, and there's a whole lot less bobbing. The voyage across the Atlantic, though, like the ship, is still epic.

***

As soon as the reservations desk opens, I get tickets for tonight's Supreme Dreamgirls performance at Headliners. We've heard good things about this show and I don't want to miss it.

Walking to the reservations desk takes more care than usual with the ship rolling about. I'm not the only one struggling to remain upright. Every other passenger I see, is holding railings as they walk. Interestingly, the unaccustomed movement does not make me feel sick. It just adds to the realization that we're in the middle of the ocean.

Staggering down the hall as the ship sways and pitches, shakes and rocks, I think of those three tiny ships that set off from Spain in 1492 searching for a path to India. The Niña, the Pinta and the Santa Maria. If our huge cruise ship with all its technological advancements can be tossed about by a lively Atlantic, what must it have been for the men on those little wooden boats with their white sails?

Here we are on the third largest cruise ship in the world, and it's bobbing around like a cork in a storm. What in the world did those courageous explorers deal with?

As I've mentioned, tickets for most onboard performances are free but the various venues are relatively small, so tickets go fast. That means we have to pay attention and get to the box office early. That is my goal for today, and fortunately, I'm able to get two tickets for tonight's performance.

The young woman behind the ticket counter is dressed up like a princess, all decked out in filmy white and topped with a silver tiara. Glittered cheeks make her whole face sparkle.

I like the playful costume. "Happy Halloween," I say.

"And a happy Halloween to you, too," she says with a smile.

Returning to our cabin, tickets in hand, I see other crew members in costume. There are pirates and witches and black cats with long tails and big ears. It's fun to see all the creativity being expressed today.

As the morning lengthens, the rough seas calm a little. But not much.

Beyond the ship's windows, the ocean is bright and roiling. Whitecaps all the way to the horizon. A molten ocean with waves fractaling and cresting and spreading out like fans or mountain ranges.

Following lunch at Taste, Al goes to the cabin for a nap and I head for Shakers Martini Bar on Deck 7.

This morning's *Freestyle Daily* announced a knitters and stitchers gathering there this afternoon and I want to see what that's all about.

KNITTERS & STITCHERS

I always learn something new on a cruise. That's probably because there's enough time on the ship for me to become familiar with it. And when a place feels familiar, I start poking around to see what else I might discover. On a cruise, it doesn't take much exploration. By glancing through the daily schedule, I can find any number of interesting things.

So, what's this gathering for knitters and stitchers?

Deck 7 has been routinely quiet and relatively empty during the day. But this afternoon, just outside of Shakers Martini Bar, the place is clicking with the sound of knitting needles and lively conversation. Every upholstered seat, every leathery couch, every bench is taken. And still women arrive with their bags of yarn and fabric.

Kitty Gonzales from central Florida has organized this group. She says she's been on six cruises.

"I love Norwegian best," she tells me. "I like the

rooms and the freestyle dining. The prices are usually really good, too. And the entertainment is great."

She's a dedicated knitter who takes her knitting projects everywhere she goes. And after a past cruise or two, she asked guest relations to announce a knitters gathering. They happily obliged.

Ever since that first gathering, she's been organizing knitters and stitchers gatherings each time she sails.

"I knew there had to be others like me who love needlework and always have a project going," she says. "And, sure enough, there were. I've held knitters and stitchers gatherings on every cruise since then."

On this cruise, it was suggested she gather her enthusiastic needle workers just outside Shaker's Martini Bar, since the place is closed during the day and provides plenty of seating in the public area surrounding the bar.

She says the group grows day by day.

"We had six our first day, then it grew to about 13 and today we've got 16 so far."

We glance around at all the women happily visiting with one another while their fingers create something beautiful. It's a warm and friendly scene.

"We meet on sea days only," Kitty says. "It's a way to do something we love and meet new friends. Sometimes men join us. Men who are into weaving or some other fabric-type art."

She says she's met knitting friends from India, Germany, Belgium, Scotland, the Netherlands, Brazil and other places through the knitting and stitching groups she's organized on cruises.

"Some of us keep in touch by email after the cruise," she says. "We send each other pictures of our projects. I do a lot of quilting, so I send pictures of my quilts."

I visit with a few others and then return to our cabin, thinking how clever Kitty Gonzales is and how generous for connecting passengers who love to knit or sew or embroider, bringing them together so they can become friends with others who share their passion. What a lovely gift she gives to them all.

***

When I reach our room, Al is ready to go to the Garden Cafe for an afternoon nosh. The ship is still rocking and rolling and we find it challenging to walk without holding onto something. So we use the railings on either side of the corridor.

Sometime overnight, the staff decorated our ship for Halloween. Pictures of skeletons and jack-o-lanterns fill the walls. And we pass more and more crew in costume. There's a festive feeling everywhere.

Despite the rough seas, the afternoon is filled with sunshine.

We savor small squares of chocolate cake as we watch the roiling ocean just beyond our Garden Cafe window. The molten gray waves carry white caps as far as I can see. It's a chilly and beautiful Atlantic.

One thing we've both appreciated on this cruise is the great movies available on our TV. Today there are two we've seen and loved: *The Help* and *March of the Penguins*. We watch a good portion of the inspiring documentary *March of the Penguins* before it's time for dinner. We saw the film twice in a theater when it first came out. And today we've watched most of it again. It never fails to thrill us.

DOING THE LAUNDRY

For me, one of the most unpleasant aspects of travel is doing the laundry. At home, a load of laundry is no big deal. But on the road, it is. If your trip is only five or six days, no problem. But longer trips pose a laundry challenge.

On past trips we've sometimes packed old undies that we could simply toss away as we traveled. That freed up space in our luggage for any souvenirs we might collect along the way. Of course, when we reached home we'd have to go shopping for underwear.

Recently, on our Mediterranean cruise, we washed our undies by hand. Not the most pleasant task, but it got the job done.

Some cruise ships have laundromats on board. We've used them and been happy with the results (although they require that you sit in the laundromat until your load is finished. Otherwise, another passenger might remove your laundry and use the machine).

The Epic has no laundromat, and it is definitely time for us to do our laundry. Our wicker hamper is full. We're nearly out of clean underclothes and still have 12 days to go before we reach home.

Although I hate to pay for it (onboard laundry and dry cleaning services are expensive), I don't want to wash all this stuff by hand.

A laundry bag hangs in our closet. We take it and its accompanying order sheet. On the sheet we list how many men's undershirts we're including, how many men's shorts, how many women's panties, how many shirts, blouses and slacks we're putting in the bag. And so on.

When we have the form filled out, Al stuffs all our dirty clothes in the bag, attaches the form, and sets it on our bed.

Our room steward will pick up the laundry when she cleans our room and will deliver it back to us when everything is clean.

[Note: To give you an idea of cruise ship laundry charges, we were billed $27.99 for our bag of laundry. While the price was steep, it was lovely to have everything clean and folded or on hangers.]

THE CASINO

Epic's casino, the biggest casino at sea, takes up much of Deck 6. In fact, in order to reach the Manhattan Dining Room, we have to walk through the casino. And, like everywhere on the Epic, the walk through is a long one.

We pass more than 300 slot machines, ranging from one-cent slots to $100 slots, on our way to dinner each day.

The casino's table games include blackjack, craps, poker, and even a Roulette wheel.

I understand that the casino offers classes for passengers (like me) who don't know how to play the various games. And throughout the cruise, there are tournaments for folks who want to try and win big.

The casino operates only when we're at sea and in international waters. For this transatlantic cruise, it's almost always open for business.

Still, as Al and I walk through each evening, we are not overwhelmed by cigarette smoke. In fact, a lot of times there's not much cigarette smoke at all. Either people are smoking less or we're simply walking through at a time when there aren't many smokers in the casino.

After reading the horrible reviews about cigarette smoke permeating the entire ship, ruining people's cruising experience, we are pleasantly surprised to encounter little or no cigarette smoke in the casino—and we haven't been bothered by it anywhere else on the ship, either.

For dinner tonight in the Manhattan, we both order baked salmon with green beans and potatoes.

Dessert is warm cherry cobbler with vanilla ice cream. Thankfully, tonight there are no substitutes for our dessert. We get exactly what we order. And we eat every bite.

SUPREME DREAMGIRLS

As soon as we finish, we're off to Headliners to try and get a good seat for the 7 p.m. show.

Unlike the huge Epic Theater, which seats 681 and has tiered seating with plush, upholstered chairs, Headliners is a more modest, intimate theater. Its 280 chairs are akin to bar chairs, tall with straight wood backs and black leather seats and they're lined up on a flat wood floor. No tiers here, so short people like me have a difficult time seeing should a tall person sit in front of us.

Headliners resembles a '70s nightclub, with brick walls, low ceilings, scuffed wood floors. A few floor-to-ceiling poles block some views.

Even though we're a half-hour early, a lot of others came earlier. We can't find two empty seats together. So I take a chair near the aisle, not too far from the stage, and Al finds a seat over on the far side of the room.

Oh, well, that'll teach us to get here earlier if we

want to sit together.

A curtain serves as the back wall of the modest stage.

When the three Supreme Dreamgirls step through the curtain in their glittering gold gowns, the room erupts with applause.

It's a fun and energetic performance, with the three vocalists giving us an evening to remember.

Their nostalgic songs include "Stop in the Name of Love," "I Will Survive," "Hit the Road, Jack," "Rollin' on the River," and "At Last My Love has Come Along."

I can't imagine that this enthusiastic trio does more than one performance a night, but they do. We simply came to the earliest one.

And we leave feeling full of happy musical memories.

THE ART GALLERY

Al returns to the room, but I want to see what's happening in the art gallery tonight.

Like many cruise lines, Norwegian has art auctions onboard, presented by Park West of Southfield, Michigan. We received an invitation to this Park West event in the art gallery this evening, an unveiling of some special work. Tonight's invitation-only event is not an auction, but I'm sure deals will be made for some of the art being revealed.

Cruise ship art auctions are fun, fast-paced and can offer decent deals on limited editions and other types of prints. Champagne flows freely and the auctioneer puts on a great show, describing each work and encouraging people to bid. Park West auctions include original paintings, one-of-a-kind drawings, etchings and limited-edition graphic works.

On past cruises, Sweetheart and I have bought limited editions by Anatole Krasnyansky and Zamy Steynovitz. We've liked the pictures and feel we received good value for what we spent. We love looking at the pictures as they hang in our home. But we knew, even as we bid on these pictures, that we were buying them because we loved them, not because they'd increase in value and make us rich.

Because I enjoy art and because we were invited to this special "unveiling of new art and artists," I'm looking forward to whatever Park West is going to present this evening.

The event starts at 9 p.m. I arrive a few minutes early, and the gallery is full of couples and individuals. Each person has a glass of champagne. I ask if the gallery has anything non-alcoholic and am soon given a glass of ginger ale.

As the program begins, we're encouraged to gather around one wall, where three large frames are draped. The Park West spokesman talks about this new artist, whose work is exciting and unique. This artist paints not only with traditional pigments, but also with liquid metal (silvers, etc.)

After the artist and his work are described, the paintings are unveiled. To me they look like something that would be in an upscale restaurant.

We move on to the next set of draped artworks, and again the Park West gallery guide gives us quite a build up to the unveiling. When the black drapes are removed, we see paintings of wine and wine glasses. What makes the works unique is the unusual angles of the glasses. One looks like we're inside a glass, gazing out. Others are equally strange to my eyes. Again, I'm not impressed. Perhaps someone who owned a winery or a restaurant would want these artworks, but I can't see hanging them in a home.

Then we're told about a set of artworks that would make major museums jealous. The art is by old, familiar, world-famous artists and is going to be sold as a four-work collection.

One by one, the pieces are brought out and placed on easels so we can get a good look at each one. An oil by Chagall, a work by Matisse, a Picasso and a Rembrandt etching. None of the works excite. Actually, I find them kind of dull.

Just a couple of weeks ago at the Rembrandt House museum in Amsterdam, Al and I saw some of the master's etchings. This etching has no energy to it at all. Of course, I'm not an art critic and don't know enough to actually criticize these works. But I know when a work of art excites me. I know when it makes me feel more alive or more aware or more happy.

And none of these works move me.

The speaker says these original works are well worth more than $100,000 but they're being offered to Epic collectors for only $29,000.

I glance around to see if anybody's eyes light up at that price, and I don't see an eager face within the crowd. Nonetheless, some couple's heads lean together as if they are sharing an idea.

Now that all the big unveilings have taken place, we're encouraged to browse the gallery and talk with any Park West person. "We're here to answer your questions," the speaker says.

I don't have any questions because we don't have any money to spend on art. But it's fun to look.

There are several colorful sculptures by Peter Max and charming oils by an array of artists. I see a Kinkade or two and some fascinating sculptures by artists whose names I don't recognize. I enjoy just strolling among the art, letting its vibrant messages surround me.

As I leave, there are still crowds studying various works or talking with Park West employees. I wonder if anyone will buy the $29,000 package.

Halloween celebrations are happening throughout the ship, as I head home. I hear the music and laughter from various lounges, and see costumed passengers or staff strolling the hallways. The masks and costumes are far less sophisticated works of art than I've just left in the gallery, but fun and engaging in their own lively way.

Riding the elevator up to our floor, I think of the two artists Park West introduced Al and me to on a long-ago cruise: Anatole Krasnyansky and Zamy Steynavitz. We would never have seen their work if we hadn't gone to a couple of Park West art auctions. Although not originals, we love the pictures of theirs that we bought. We have limited edition serigraphs that brighten up rooms in our home.

While cruise ship art auctions are fun, they can add thousands to your bill. So it's only wise to do a little research before you plunk down your money. From the start we had the rule that we'd only buy something if we truly loved it. And that's what we've done. So we've never felt cheated.

When I tell Al about the $29,000 package, he just rolls his eyes.

The Manhattan Dining Room.

NOV. 1 - VISITING WITH EXECUTIVE CHEF KEVIN GREEN

We awaken to much calmer seas. A welcome change. I wonder how many passengers suffered from seasickness yesterday.

Well before breakfast, Al takes his camera out on deck to photograph clouds. You might think being surrounded with ocean for as far as you can see in all directions would result in somewhat boring scenery. But for an artist or photographer or anyone with a sensitive eye, the colors and textures surrounding our ship change continually. It's a challenge to try to capture the beauty of sea and sky on film, a challenge Al relishes.

This morning clouds hang down from the sky like long, fluffy strips of cotton. The sun paints them gold in places, stunning white in others.

Breakfast is a quick bite in the Garden Cafe. Then Al is off exploring with his camera and I prepare for my appointment with Executive Chef Kevin Green.

The executive chef is in charge of the entire food operation in all the outlets throughout the ship, from the buffet and pool grill to the traditional dining rooms and the many specialty dining venues. The food and beverage team alone numbers about 880.

The main hot galley on Deck 5 is where the meals for the Manhattan Dining Room and Taste Dining Room are prepared.

The specialty restaurants have their own galleys.

The pantry, a station in the galley, is where cold appetizers, salads, sandwiches and other cold items for the lunch and dinner buffets are prepared.

There are fish, meat and poultry stations, a bakery, and dessert and pastry area. And the executive chef is responsible for them all.

After the breakfast crush and before lunch rush, I meet Kevin Green at a table in the Manhattan Dining Room. The large restaurant at the back of the ship is empty and quiet.

Chef Green has coffee and cream delivered to our table as we chat.

Although he has worked as a chef for nearly 30 years, Kevin Green looks disarmingly young with his full head of dark hair, his unwrinkled face and his bright eyes behind glasses.

Born and raised in Costa Rica, he says the TV show The Love Boat captured his youthful imagination.

"I loved that show. It gave me my goal in life—to become a bartender on a cruise ship," he says with a laugh.

In college, cooking was a required class. And he says his family expected him to cook for them. Although at first he didn't like cooking, he grew to enjoy it.

At 20, he landed a cruise ship job as a bar tender. He grins as he describes achieving his life's ambition at such a young age. While tending bar, he got acquainted with crew members who worked in the galley and he decided that galley work would be more interesting than bartending.

So he quit his "dream job" and returned to college. His professors recognized his talent and encouraged him. He finished his education with a culinary degree. He worked as a pastry cook. He won some competitions.

"I met the right chef to coach me and guide me," he says. "I learned German cooking and French cooking."

His first job with Norwegian Cruise Lines was as a galley steward.

"I helped out in the kitchen for a couple of months, and then the German chef started me in the cold kitchen making salads."

Through the years, he worked the pastry and bake shops, the butcher shop, learned soup and sauce making.

"I grew my career in this company," he says with a hint of pride in his voice.

In 1998 he was promoted to working chef in charge of the buffet. Three years later, he was promoted again. And in 2004 he was named Executive Chef.

"I used to be shy," he says. "My first language is Spanish. My grandma was from Jamaica. I think some of that contributed to my shyness, but being in this position has given me more confidence."

Chef Green is responsible for cooks, galley stewards and station heads. He works directly with seven sous chefs who oversee all the various culinary details onboard.

"We meet daily to keep us all on the same page," he says.

In addition to feeding the passengers, Chef

Green plans menus for the crew. "We prepare the crews' meals—foods from the Philippines, the Caribbean, India, Indonesia. They each have different seasonings. We also have European and USA crew members to cook for."

I ask him about the daily consumption on this transatlantic cruise. He says we passengers are eating about 600 pounds of bacon a day.

"Europeans don't care much for bacon, but Americans want it," he says.

He's using 600 pounds of flour a day, 900 pounds of fresh potatoes a day, 6,000 dozen fresh eggs each day. That includes breakfast eggs—fried, scrambled, etc.—and all the eggs used in baked goods.

"Cooking is about passion," he says. "I cook for 4,000 guests and 1,700 crew members. When I cook and the people are happy, it's the best."

He says the meals for each dining venue are planned well ahead of cruise time. The corporate office designs the menus and Chef Green orders the ingredients.

"Sometimes we don't have (or can't get) what we need, so then I make some changes," he says. "We have to be creative especially for the buffet. For the buffet we prepare dishes from Spain, Italy, Asia and the Mediterranean. We have different desserts every day at the buffet. And we prepare our large salad bar daily."

He says Norwegian passengers eat a lot of steak. "Prime ribs are one of the most popular choices on this cruise," he says. "On one night, we served 1,100 prime ribs." He laughs at the thought and shakes his head.

"For the first seven days of a cruise, people eat a lot. They eat everything. Sometimes two of everything. After that, they begin to slow down."

I ask why he thinks they slow down.

"Their clothes are getting too tight!" He laughs heartily.

He says the most challenging food on a long cruise is fresh produce. He bought a lot of fresh berries for this cruise and a lot of frozen berries.

"My fresh berries are holding up well," he says. "But the frozen berries will finish off the cruise."

Long cruises, like this transatlantic cruise, are filled with older folks, he says. "Older people eat early," he says. "They have medications to take with their dinner." He says we older folks eat significantly more vegetables. "I have to order plenty of fresh vegetables. They eat more salads, more fruits, more broccoli, more cauliflower."

He says it's completely different on cruises during spring break. "That's all French fries and burgers," he says with a grin.

About special dietary needs, he says, "I receive special diet orders four weeks before the cruise. We prepare gluten-free, lactose-free, vegetarian, kosher and other special types of menus. It's our job to cook for our guests, to give them the best vacation ever."

He tells me about a family whose children had all sorts of food allergies.

"We didn't find out until the second day, but then I personally took over their cooking. I didn't rest at all the week they were onboard, but I felt good and so proud of myself because I could prepare the kind of meals they needed," he says.

"I became like the uncle for the whole family. That was five years ago and they still keep in touch with me."

Clearly, he not only loves to cook, but he also loves the passengers he cooks for.

"I love people," he says. "And when they like my food and my management, I'm happy."

As we part, Chef Green gives me what he calls a

typical weekly shopping list. Here's what's on it:

cereal – 2,000 lbs.

butter – 3,600 lbs.

pasta – 1,500 lbs.

cheese – 5,500 lbs.

fresh fruit – 38,000 lbs.

sugar – 3,900 lbs.

fresh eggs – 5,600 dozen (72,200 eggs)

fish – 8,700 lbs.

veal – 1,000 lbs.

lobster – 1,000 lbs.

poultry – 1,400 lbs.

beef – 15,000 lbs.

ice cream – 1,000 gallons

soft ice cream – 6,000 lbs.

seafood – 2,600 lbs.

yogurt – 4,500 lbs.

coffee – 2,300 lbs.

vegetables – 30,000 lbs.

milk – 1,600 gallons

rice – 7,500 lbs.

potatoes –13,000 lbs.

flour – 10,000 lbs.

wine – 150 different kinds

Nov. 1 - Visiting with Executive Chef Kevin Green

Here's where the crowds hang out each day.

NOV. 2 - MEETING THE CAPTAIN AND CREW

We're more than halfway through this transatlantic cruise. I can't believe this is our eighth day on board already.

The old cliché, "When you're having fun, time just seems to fly," has certainly been true for me on this trip.

Today we share a calm and leisurely breakfast at Taste. Al has orange juice, a muffin, half a grapefruit (it came with sections of mandarin orange tucked in between the sections of grapefruit, very pretty) and smoked salmon on a bagel. He says it's an A+ breakfast.

My orange juice, croissant, sliced banana and veggie omelet are also A+.

While we linger over our coffee, I study the *Freestyle Daily* and see that at 10 a.m. in Headliners there's a "Meet the Captain & Crew" event.

"You want to go?" I ask. He shakes his head.

Well, I certainly want to go. I want to hear what

it's like running a floating city with issues as varied as medical care, waste disposal, safety and more. This should be very informative.

I get to Headliners 15 minutes before the event and the place is packed. But I find an empty chair near the front. I probably got the last available seat.

Three men in crisp white uniforms sit on stools on the stage: Chief Engineer Geir Saether, Hotel Director Richard Janicki, and Captain Frank Levi Andreas Juliussen. Each man introduces himself and talks briefly about his job, his training and when he joined Norwegian Cruise Line.

Then they open the floor for questions or comments. The first question concerns the medical emergency that took place when we were near Madeira.

Captain Juliussen says, "Life and safety are our highest priority, so we contacted a shoreside rescue center. I turned the ship around and headed back. At the time our speed was low so we could afford to change direction."

He says that the woman who was airlifted by helicopter is doing OK.

Someone asks how much ship's fuel was used for the airlift rescue. He says, "240 tons."

The audience is not shy. The questions fly.

Question: How far can the ship go on a gallon of fuel?

Captain Juliussen: We average two feet a gallon.

Question: How often do you have to test the life boats?

Captain Juliussen: Every week we have crew drills. We lower life boats on each side down to the water. By law they must be in the water once a week.

Question: How many people can a lifeboat hold?

Captain Juliussen: We have 20 lifeboats. Twelve hold 293 persons each. Eight tender boats hold 267 persons each. So we have lifeboat capacity for 5,652 individuals. We also have two rescue boats and 19 life rafts. Each life raft holds 158 persons.

There's a question about onboard sewage treatment. And Chief Engineer Saether says the ship has about 3.5 thousand tons of waste a day.

"The food waste is ground up and released into the ocean as fish food," he says. "We have a city sewage plant onboard. The clear, treated water goes overboard. The solids go to a sludge tank to be dried and later incinerated."

Several questions concern food. How much is taken onboard for a cruise like ours? What's disappearing fastest? Questions like that.

Hotel Manager Janicki says the ship took on enough provisions of food and drink to fill 20 40-foot-long trucks.

"You're doing a good job with your food consumption," he says. "You're doing exceptionally well with the ice cream."

Everyone laughs.

Then he elaborates: "You're eating between 700 and 800 pounds of ice cream every day."

Someone asks if the ship uses solar power. Captain Juliussen says, "We use it for laundry. We're looking at solar for more electrical uses."

There are many questions about the ship itself. The captain says it has fixed propellers, two rudders and two storm thrusters.

"Two knots is the minimum speed for the rudders to work. I prefer working on big ships because they have more safety equipment. And as far as stability goes (I know we had some rough water earlier in the week), it has a lot to do with weight distribution. The Epic's steel thickness is twice what smaller ships have. And our weight is very low."

The Epic contains 77 million pounds of steel. "That's the equivalent of 28,000 mid-size cars," he says. "The Epic's electrical cables would stretch 1,740 miles."

Someone asks about the anchor. Captain Juliussen says there are two anchors and a spare. "Each anchor weighs 16,125 tons," he says. A murmur fills the room. A mostly masculine murmur.

As the gathering continues, passengers begin voicing complaints. The most common from the men is the cost and sluggishness of the Internet service.

Hotel Manager Janicki says, "I can only encourage patience. And a lot of it. On land you can get Internet in the blink of an eye. But we don't have a cable trailing behind us on our cruises. We hope in the future that our technology can be better. I'm sorry it's so slow, but this is how it is right now."

The most common complaint from the women is the low level of lighting in the cabins.

"You can't see a thing. Can't put on makeup," many women say.

Again, there are apologies. But the lighting is the way it's going to be.

Several people complain about other people saving (or reserving) poolside lounges by putting a towel or a book or a hat on them. According to ship rules, passengers are not supposed to save such lounges for more than 30 minutes. But they do. They "save" lounges sometimes for hours. "They're not supposed to do that," several voices say.

People want the captain or the hotel manager to enforce the rules.

Hotel Manager Janicki nods sympathetically. "It is a problem," he concedes. "And crew members do not want to anger passengers. They want everyone to have a good time, a happy time. So they're unlikely to chastise a passenger who is breaking the rule."

He pauses, then says, "We have to do a better job of urging guests to be polite."

As I leave, I think about the complaints. It is true that passengers are inconsiderately selfish when they reserve a lounge near the pools or on the sun deck but don't use it for hours. It sits vacant while someone else could (and would like to) use it.

If I really wanted a lounge chair, and one had sat empty for an hour, I think I'd simply remove the towel and claim the lounge for myself.

If someone is not obeying the rules of the ship, and I really want to lie in the sun, would I be selfish to simply claim the vacant lounge as my own?

If the original person returned and was unhappy

with me, I'd gently say that the lounge had been vacant for an hour, so I assumed it was free. And then I'd just as gently remind the passenger that the rule is, you can only reserve a lounge chair for 30 minutes. Or would that be rubbing it in a little too much?

And as for the dim room lighting, it's true. There is no bright light above the makeup table. Actually, the only bright lights in our room are the reading lights on either side of the bed. I find the low lighting restful. But then, I don't use much makeup. If I did, I'd certainly find it difficult to apply eye liner or other kinds of makeup. To apply artful makeup, I guess I'd go to one of the public restrooms scattered about the ship. They have excellent lighting and large mirrors.

Of course, it's always easy to solve problems when they're not your own, isn't it. I wonder if the captain and crew hear the same complaints every time they meet with passengers.

I can see that a meeting like this can help passengers feel closer to the captain and crew. It would be nice to think the complaints and suggestions offered by the passengers lead to changes.

***

Following lunch in the Garden Cafe (roast beef sandwich for Al, chicken Thai stir fry for me), we go up to the pool deck and find chairs in the shade where we can read, daydream or write.

It's 78 degrees. The ocean is an easy blue rising and falling as if it's breathing under a pale sky filled with powdery white clouds. In the background I hear the plunk plunk plunk of a ping-pong game, punctuated by male voices yelling, "Oh!" or "All Riiiight!"

OUR CONCERN ABOUT CROWDS

It is true that 4,000 cruisers (plus staff and crew) make for a full ship. And although the picture of crowds squeezing each other in a sardine can crush is not entirely accurate, at times here on the Epic it seems we're always in a crowd.

I can only say this: crowding depends on the time of day and the location onboard. Pool areas always seem to be packed during sunlight hours. But there are many less crowded, quiet places throughout the ship where you can sit and read, play cards (or in our case, Scrabble), enjoy a drink or even a nap.

One of the distinct benefits of such a large ship is

the wide variety of activities available. We've cruised on several lines and never before have we had a genuine water park or climbing wall onboard.

Although I'm disappointed in the pathetic library, the ship plays recently released movies on the TV, and good movies on Spice H2O's outdoor screen. Sometimes, there are movies playing on the huge screen in the atrium.

Here are a few of the films being shown on this cruise: *Apollo 13, The Help, 42* (the Jackie Robinson story), *The Monuments Men,* and for those of us who enjoy classic flicks: *Rear Window* with Grace Kelly, James Stewart and Raymond Burr.

Daily activities are numerous: from Sudoku on the big screen in the atrium, to bowling, calligraphy classes, dance classes and ice carving demonstrations. There are special group meetings such as the knitters and stitchers group I attended. There are Friends of Bill W. meetings, Friends of Dorothy meetings, solo traveler gatherings and various tournaments in the casino.

Youngsters and teens have an array of their own activities. To give you an idea of the youth this cruise line serves, the TV show *Nickelodeon* is broadcast in Spanish and German as well as English.

And here we are on a sunny Sunday afternoon, in a quiet nook enjoying the sea.

Not far from us, a bearded, white-haired man in a turquoise tank top, black shorts and flip-flops is reading a book. A couple closer to the railing have spread out their Norwegian beach towels. The wife sits on a lounge. The husband—bald, round and barefoot—sits beside her in a chair. He has another chair facing him, forming a kind of reading lounge. They're both reading tablets.

A bit farther down the deck, two elderly gentlemen are playing a game of chess. The two-foot-tall chess pieces have to be moved by walking onto the board and moving them.

And not far beyond them is the rock climbing wall. Although no one's climbing the wall, there are definitely people enjoying the green giant curlicue of a water slide. They come shooting down the curving slide and land with a giant splash in a trough of water. From the laughter and repeats, it's clear the experience is loads of fun.

All of these activities and all these people, but I do not feel crowded as we sit and read in our little out-of-the-way space. The warm air holds us affectionately. A shadow protects us from the sun and yet we have an unobstructed view of the endless ocean, its beauty both calming and reassuring.

AL AND THE WATER SLIDE

It was another perfect day at sea: blue sky; blue water; warm, soft air. We'd been reading on the pool deck, but decided to visit the Garden Cafe buffet. It had been easily two hours since we'd last eaten, an unconscionable amount of time. Supper lay on the distant horizon, easily an hour and a half away: much too far.

A plate of something sweet (remember: sugar is a food group), taken outside to the Aqua Park was definitely in order.

The pool—actually, the entire ship's Aqua Park— was packed with humanity. It was as if the entire passenger contingent aboard the Epic had decided it was a perfect day to frolic in the sun. All that pink flesh slowly turning red, like chicken legs turning on a rotisserie's grill. Definitely a sight to behold. There wouldn't be a bottle of aloe lotion left in the ship's store by evening, but in the here-and-now no one cared.

Being of senior years (though not always of senior wisdom), I'm not much into frolicking. And yet ... as we sat and enjoyed our snacks, the sheer ebullience of *the throng swept over me. I couldn't just sit there and let this beautiful day pass. It was time to dash back to our stateroom and put on my swimming trunks. Which I did.*

Since this was the first time my body had been exposed to sunlight in considerable time, I knew that lying in the sun was not a wise idea. The pool was filled with eager children; the hot tub filled with ... let us say ... larger individuals.

Being neither a kid nor a whale, I wondered where to go. The answer was obvious: the water slide.

The Epic actually has three slides, twisting their way high above the deck. The largest—and tallest— is a 200-foot-long, four-story-high tube that plunges into a giant bowl. It looked like a lot of fun.

I remembered the time that Sunny and I had gone to a water park near our home in California. It had been wonderful; even exciting. The long climb up the stairs: sitting down on the inner tube: tearing down the slide into the catch basin.

Of course, that was a few years back. One—no, two—heart attacks ago. A time when both knees worked.

What the heck, I thought. You're only as old as your spirit. Right?

Up the steps I went, somewhat more slowly than those behind might have wanted, until I stood at the landing atop the Epic's biggest water slide.

And then I saw The Sign.

I wasn't wearing my reading glasses, but I didn't need them. The sign, in large print and unambiguous language, specified who was ineligible to go down the slide. Children smaller than a certain size. People uncomfortable in small enclosed places (the slide is a tube). And those with certain medical problems, particularly problems of a coronary nature. Hmmm.

Decision time. I was sure my ticker would keep ticking if I took the plunge, so to speak, but a look from my wife said it all.

Back down the steps, to the dismay of those ascending. Call me a wuss if you will, but given a choice between being a wuss or being happily married, I'll opt for my bride every time. Easy decision.

I don't remember what we did the rest of the afternoon, there by the pool, but I know we had a great time. We left before we got sunburned and went back to our cabin, where we took a nap. It was a wonderful day.

Seafood night in the Garden Cafe.

NOV. 3 - A CONVERSATION WITH EPIC'S HOTEL DIRECTOR

Day nine of our 14-day ocean cruise. The weather is as it has been all trip long: perfect. Well, except for the day we were rocking and rolling.

After breakfast, we ride the elevator to Deck 15 where we enjoyed reading yesterday afternoon. When we step off, we hear the energetic beat of exercising music. And as we pass the pools, we see dozens of people dancing and moving in time to the music. Their early-morning energy makes us feel a little guilty. We should really join them. But the guilt passes quickly.

At the outer deck we find chairs to sit and read in. A tranquil breeze skims across the waves, ruffling the pages of my journal and Al's beautiful white hair.

We read until about 11:30 when we head for the theater to watch the noon performance of magician Christian Miro. It will be a close-up magic show.

My brother is a close-up magician. For years he performed at Hollywood's Magic Castle. Now he works independently as a comedic magician. I've loved his various acts over the years and whenever I hear about a magician I want to watch and see what he does, and if he does any of the illusions my talented brother performs.

Al and I have heard good things about Christian Miro from others on the ship.

We arrive at the theater 20 minutes early and people are already filling the seats. Frank Sinatra's voice sings "That Old Black Magic," perfect background music for a magic show.

The woman in the seat next to me says she saw Christian's act last night and it was spectacular. She says it was so good she's here today and plans to go see his evening show again. That excites me.

I love magic acts. Love being wowed! I'm not one of those people who tries to figure out how the magician does his tricks. I just want to be caught up in the wonder of it all. Watching things disappear and reappear. It's fun to be amazed!

Christian Miro comes out on stage wearing a black business suit. He stands behind a table covered in a royal blue cloth. Video cameras focus on the table top where his hands will perform their magic. And above the stage are huge screens where we can watch his hands as if we were only a few inches from him.

He introduces himself, explaining that he is from Madrid and that's why he speaks English with an accent. He's stocky, with a full head of curly black hair, although he laments a thinning spot on top. His smile is bright and warm as he launches into his act.

From card and coin tricks, to magic ball tricks and other illusions, he keeps us staring at the large TV screens, trying to see where the disappearing coins go and how the magic balls multiply right before our eyes. He makes playing cards float from the deck, or a specific card rise to the top of the deck repeatedly, no matter where it is placed inside the other cards.

It's all wonderful and mystifying. The audience gasps and laughs and claps. He's funny and charming in the most natural of ways. He seems to be having as much fun performing as we're having watching him.

All too quickly, the show is finished and he's inviting us to come to his evening performance, a much longer show. We have tickets to a comedy hypnotist program tonight, but I'll watch the

Freestyle Daily newsletter to find when he has another evening show, and we'll definitely be there for it.

RICHARD JANICKI, EPIC'S HOTEL DIRECTOR

After a quick bite in the Garden Cafe, I make my way to the Hotel Director's office. Richard Janicki welcomes me. His office is a comfortable room with a desk and file cabinet. He's a confident officer with brown eyes, a receding hairline and a generous smile.

He says he knew since he was a child living in France that when he grew up he wanted to work in a big hotel. And he did. He worked as a cook in high-end hotels in several countries. He learned the business ins and outs. And today he's responsible for one of the biggest floating resorts on the world's oceans.

"I'm responsible for everything," he says with a laugh. "All 1,708 crew members report to me."

He talks about expecting the crew to give passengers top quality service.

"Guests may have saved their money for years to buy a cruise for some special occasion like an anniversary. And we want them to have the greatest anniversary. We have to be good for them right now. We don't get reruns. Now is when they're here celebrating."

I ask what the difference is between people who are on this 14-day transatlantic cruise and folks who take typical seven-day cruises.

"They're older. And on a cross Atlantic cruise you must be prepared to relax, to get pampered. We're here to take care of you, so rest, slow down, sink into serenity."

Then his eyes twinkle and he says, "But have some fun too. Take a dance class. Show off what you can do in the passenger talent show."

I ask what cultural differences he's noticed among passengers on this cruise.

"American's like their cocktails," he says. "Europeans like beer and wine. The British want gin and tonic."

When Mr. Janicki is not taking care of everything on the ship, he makes his home in Greece.

But this afternoon he wants to talk about the Epic. It's obvious that he thinks the Epic is the greatest cruise ship in the world.

"What sets us apart is our freestyle cruising. It all

started with dining whenever you like. Traditionally, cruise ships offer two seatings in a main dining room. And they also have the buffet.

"We changed that, offering many dining options. You can eat whenever you want in any number of places. There are no fixed dining times. We offer more choices and less regimentation.

"And now our freestyle culture includes entertainment. Traditionally, cruises offered one big show in the main theater. You could go to the early show or the late show.

"We've designed several smaller venues, with lots of different kinds of shows every night. You have many choices. And our shows are repeated so if you miss something you really wanted to see, you'll have a chance to catch it later."

He emphasizes the quality of the Epic's entertainment and entertainers.

"We have name performers like The Blue Man Group and Legends," he says. "And one nice thing about having smaller entertainment venues is that when the show is over you aren't caught in a throng of thousands trying to get out of the theater and back to your room."

I mention the downside of having to make

reservations and get tickets for the smaller venues, a task that irritates some. He just raises his eyebrows and shrugs. Obviously, every innovation has its pros and cons and he wants to emphasize the pros.

I ask about the curving walls of our inside cabin, and the reason for splitting up the bathroom.

"We wanted to get away from the square, boxy feeling," he says. "I think the curving walls give more closet space. Don't you?"

I have to admit, they do. Our closet could almost be described as "walk in."

And the bathroom arrangement, he says, frees up the room for more than one person at a time.

"On a traditional cruise ship, if someone is showering, no one else can use the bathroom. But with our floor plan, someone can be showering, and the toilet is still available, and the sink can still be used to brush your teeth or whatever," he says. "Some people love the layout. Others don't."

He asks me if I've been bothered by smoke from the casino. I haven't. He says, "We've reduced the smoking space in the casino. We listen to guest concerns, and we respond by improving things."

He says the Epic is a great cruise ship for families. "We have activities for grandkids, for parents and grandparents. The whole extended family can cruise together and have a good time."

The newest innovation he wants to talk about is the studio cabins for solo passengers. Pioneered by Norwegian, these studio cabins are designed and priced for the solo traveler.

Traditionally, solo passengers had to reserve a regular-sized room and pay a supplemental fee of 20 to 50 percent for it. Or they had to find a friend to join them and split the cost.

Epic's solo cabins are priced more reasonably, Janicki says. And they come with a private studio complex and lounge. In the lounge, passengers can watch big screen TV, can enjoy complimentary coffee, espresso drinks, snacks and can socialize with other solo travelers.

"Forget classic cruising," he says. "Free style is everything. On Epic, do your homework, think about when and how you want to eat, which shows you want to see and then go with the flow. That's the beauty of it. You don't have to commit to a specific time or a specific restaurant."

Richard Janicki is a busy man and I'm grateful for his time this afternoon. As he walks me out of his office, I wish we'd had time to talk about the ship's brig and morgue.

Although I didn't ask, I know that each cruise ship has a brig (jail cell) for problem passengers and a morgue for those who die onboard. I'm curious if Epic has more brig and morgue space because of its large passenger capacity. I'll just assume the answer is "yes."

***

Dinner in the Manhattan. Al orders French onion soup and spring greens salad. He rates it an A+ dinner.

I have spring greens salad, Curried Thai shrimp with rice and broccoli. Also an A+.

He has cafe crème for dessert, a coffee-flavored custard, which he describes as, "So good, I could easily eat two more."

I have a "warm chocolate volcano" with a side of vanilla gelato and strawberry compote. Way too rich for me to eat the whole thing.

There are so many choices on the dinner menu that we can have something different each night and never get through all the offerings even in two weeks.

Following dinner, it's off to the theater to see

comedy hypnotist Nadeen. In the elevator we meet a woman from the UK. I ask if she's enjoying the cruise.

"Yes," she says enthusiastically. "A long cruise with lots of sea days is so relaxing isn't it?"

Al and I agree. As I've said before, I love sea days when we just float along and I have all the unscheduled time I want to daydream or read or explore the ship.

Although the theater is pretty full when we arrive, we find two good seats and settle in to enjoy the show.

And a strange show it is. Dressed all in black, with skintight slacks and super-tall spikes, Nadeen looks like a model. Her black hair, full and hanging well below her shoulders, frames her face beautifully. Strutting back and forth across the stage, she exudes confidence. She promises to entertain and empower us.

With the help of assistants, she chooses 20 or more volunteers from the audience and seats them side by side in a stage-wide line of chairs. Then she hypnotizes the group and leads them through various exercises.

As the volunteers try to relax (can you imagine

actually relaxing on stage in front of an entire theater full of people staring at you?), she directs them to raise their arms, or sing or sleep or do other things.

There are some very funny episodes during the show, but all in all Al and I are not as entertained as we are aghast. Nothing seems genuine. It all seems fake. The volunteers seem to be pretending. Perhaps it's a poor night for volunteers. I don't know. But we whisper about leaving early and decide to stay and see if things improve. They don't.

However, Nadeen says her volunteers are super. She announces that she's offering more personalized seminars during the cruise. She invites audience members to attend her the seminars where for a fee they can get help with problems such as losing weight or stopping smoking. She promises that her seminars are revitalizing and empowering.

After the show, we swing by the Atrium Cafe and split a chocolaty muffin as we sip decaf lattes. A sweet and satisfying end to the day.

Pulse Fitness Center on Deck 14 is open daily.

NOV. 4 - ANOTHER DAY AT SEA

At breakfast we share our table with a couple from England who have been traveling on Norwegian for more than 20 years. Meg and Thomas say they love the line because it is casual.

"You don't have to dress up," Thomas says. "No formal nights. It's great to be able to dress in shorts and T-shirts all cruise long. But I'll tell you something I don't like. The crowded sun decks. It's almost impossible to get a sun lounge."

Just like us, this is their first time on a mega-ship, and there are certain things that they definitely do not like.

Meg doesn't like having to make reservations for evening entertainment. "And it really disturbs me when we can't get a seat because all the tickets are already gone," she says. "Yes it's nice to have many choices, but if you're slow on getting your tickets, you might be totally shut out of a show you wanted to see."

I mentioned what Hotel Director Janicki had told me, that shows run more than once during a cruise, but that information doesn't seem to soften Meg's opinion.

Then both she and Thomas perked up as they told us about The Blue Man Group that they'd seen. "It was a great act!" they both said. So great, in fact, that they'd go see it again.

Our breakfast conversation ends on this positive note.

Al and I have been meaning all cruise long to check out the Pulse Fitness Center on Deck 14. This is the gym where we should be working out every day.

As we leave Taste, we decide to do it now. And off we go. The fitness center turns out to be way at the back of the ship and we have to walk through a "residential" area (nothing but staterooms) and then through the spa area, but when we finally reach it, we are impressed.

The fitness center is large and inviting. Its treadmills are lined up so that they face the floor-to-ceiling windows looking out on the ocean. The view is both restful and inspiring.

In addition to treadmills, there are stationary

bicycles, rowing machines, weights and boxing bags. And an area with mats for yoga or other exercises.

We'd thought we might do a little exercising this morning, but the place is full and busy. Walkers ranging from youthful athletes wearing spandex to older folks in shorts and T-shirts stride energetically on the treadmills. Rowing machines and bicycles are equally occupied.

On other cruises, Al and I have been daily exercisers. And often when walking or rowing or weight lifting, we had the gym mostly to ourselves. But on this cruise we've been more sedentary. Too bad that the day we finally decide to go to the gym, it's too full for us. Oh well, we'll just have to go find ourselves a latte and a good book.

In about an hour, we'll wander down to the Epic Theater to hear Beatles classics sung by a look-alike group.

One thing I've enjoyed on this cruise is the mid-day entertainment. I've never before been on a cruise with shows in the middle of the day.

Al says he'd prefer a soft ice cream to a latte. So we go to Deck 15 where a soft ice cream machine exists. I get a little paper cup of vanilla and chocolate mixed together in a beautiful and delicious swirl. Al fills a cone with chocolate. We find a shaded table for two not far from the pool and enjoy our sweet treat.

I love the soft breeze, and the background babble of all the vacation conversations. Whether eating his ice cream or reading his Kindle, Al's silvery hair and white beard making him appear both handsome and wise.

Not far from us, a young father with his baby boy (I'm sure the child is less than a year old) heads for the grill area. He's carrying his diapered son in one arm, and the bright little guy smiles and waves over his dad's shoulder.

As with most of the eating areas onboard, a crew member with a disinfectant squirt bottle stands ready to squirt the hands of those who enter. The dad says, "Hold out your hand," and the baby holds out his chubby hand. The crew member squirts it and the child giggles. The dad gets his hands sprayed and starts to move on, but the child cries and holds out his hand again. The crew member squirts it and the little boy giggles. He holds out his hand again, gets another squirt and giggles. This routine goes on for a while, until the baby tires and the dad heads for the grill.

I find the scene endearing—the baby's delight,

the dad's patience, and the amused crew member, happy to fulfill the little one's desire.

I watch as the dad and son go through the line, the dad getting a hamburger, a small bowl of chips, and a drink. At a table, after setting the tray down, he carefully fits the child into a plastic high chair and puts a chip in each little hand. Then he sits down to enjoy his burger and drink.

The baby chomps away on a chip. Then he notices two grandmotherly women at the next table, and holds out his half eaten chip. One of the women smiles and accepts his gift.

The baby's face glows with happiness.

I'm so glad I got to watch all the discoveries this baby boy made today on a giant cruise ship in the middle of the Atlantic Ocean. He won't remember these charming moments, but I will.

Not far from us, another table holds three young males, all tanned and toned and youthfully gorgeous, consuming large platters of pineapple, water melon and other fresh fruits. The pink and yellow slices are perfect colors on this gentle afternoon.

At other tables, people play cards and sip cool drinks.

Not far from us, a group of women play Mahjong,

their tiles clicking loudly on the table top.

While there are lots of people here, it doesn't feel like there's too many. Rather than feeling crowded, I feel included in a friendly atmosphere warmed by the sun.

At 12:30 the Epic Theater is filling up fast, but we find two good seats and settle in to enjoy some music from our past.

By the time the Beatles Celebration Live! concert starts at 1 p.m. every seat is taken and people are sitting on the steps and standing around the walls.

When the fab four take the stage, the place becomes electric. They look like the Beatles and they sound like the Beatles and their energy radiates until we all feel young and full of vigor.

There's virtually no patter, just song after wonderful song: "Help," "She Loves You," "Hey Jude," and many others.

So much energy! So much enthusiasm!

The audience cannot stay seated. We're clapping and stomping and singing along. The whole concert is exhilarating!

The couple next to me are from Scotland and they bring a feeling of "These guys are our guys" to our row. The woman says they've cruised many times, have been to New York, Florida and San Francisco, but it's clear they love being right here, singing with the Beatles in the middle of the ocean.

Once the concert ends, we return to our room for a luxurious afternoon nap.

***

After dinner in the Manhattan (linguine with clams for Al, roast chicken breast and broccoli for me), I head for the theater to enjoy the magician we'd seen earlier in the week. Al doesn't feel good, so he's staying in tonight.

"The Comedy Magic of Christian Miro," is thoroughly entertaining. Much of it is familiar as he does classic magic tricks—metal rings that link and unlink mysteriously, rope that is cut into several different lengths and then magically restored to wholeness and numerous playing card illusions.

Yet he puts his own spin on these tricks and wraps them in humor. He seems concerned about losing hair, and many times during his act he asks the audience if his hair looks all right. We, of course, applaud and shout that he looks great.

The question and response gets louder and

funnier each time it is repeated.

He also adds some hilarious ventriloquisms to the act.

By the end of the show, I'm thinking that Christian Miro is both talented and wonderful. He entertains us by proving right before our eyes that the impossible is possible. And he makes us laugh with his corny jokes and self-deprecating humor.

Afterwards, as I walk back to our room, I count off the shows we've seen onboard.

1. Cirque Dreams & Dinner, which was exciting and unforgettable.
2. Supreme Dreamgirls, which was quite good.
3. The Beatles celebration, which felt fantastic.
4. Christine Miro's magic and humor, which I love.
5. Nadeen's comedy hypnotism, which we didn't care for.

That's a lot of fun entertainment. And we still have time for more on this cruise.

A few of our friends back home feel that cruise ship entertainment is less than top rate. But I don't.

Over the years I've been to Broadway shows

and Las Vegas shows. I've seen performers in San Francisco and Los Angeles. And I think the Beatles tribute band we saw today was top rate. And the Cirque Dreams and Dinner show was every bit as exciting as a Cirque du Soleil performance on land.

Of course, not every performance will please all people. If you don't like magic, don't bother with a magic show. If you don't like big musical productions, skip the big musical show. But with all the variety available on this cruise, surely there will be something entertaining for everyone. More than one something.

***

Back in our room, Al is thumbing through a list of shore excursions. After so many days at sea, he's eager to get off the ship and wander around a little.

When we dock in the morning, it will have been seven days since we last set foot on land. At that time it was Funchal on the island of Madeira, with its cliffs rising half-way to heaven.

Tomorrow we'll visit the smallest land mass in the world to be shared by two different nations: France and the Netherlands.

The French side of this 37-square-mile island

is called Saint Martin. The Dutch side is called Sint Maarten. Between these two independently governed territories there is no border patrol, no customs, no fences.

And, as with every port of call, the ship offers shore excursions. On most cruises, including this one, shore excursion tours cost extra. Sometimes a lot extra.

So it's important to know what you value. If you prefer to stroll through shops or walk the streets with your camera at your own pace, you probably won't want to spend money on a shore excursion. But if you want a guide to show you the sights, to explain the history of the area, or to take you through museums or historic churches, you may want to buy a shore excursion.

Al and I have taken great shore excursions: to see the Acropolis in Athens before the tourist crowds arrive, to visit a sea horse farm in Hawaii, and in Funchal our breathtaking bus tour took us to the top of the highest cliff in Europe. That was something we would never have done on our own.

So Al is checking out the tours available for tomorrow.

He's interested in a bicycle tour that starts at 2

p.m. I can't imagine his wanting to peddle around the island with his hurting knees. But he assures me that the tour description makes it sound like everything's on level ground. "Just a couple of slight inclines," he says. I wonder exactly what "slight inclines" means, but he quickly adds, "And I could use the exercise after all these days and desserts."

He loves to ride his bike back home. He goes to the grocery or to his darkroom/studio. But those are relatively short rides. However, I refrain from voicing my concern.

All I'm interested in doing tomorrow is swimming at one of the beautiful white sand beaches. I don't care for the heat of the Caribbean; it's way too hot for me. But swimming in the clear blue ocean waters is the best experience ever. I can float among the gentle swells "forever."

In the list of excursions I find one called "The Best of Sint Maarten Scenic Drive and Beach." The beach this tour goes to is on Orient Bay, a clothing-optional beach. So, maybe I'll see some nude bathers. In Florence and Rome, we saw lots of nude statues, both male and female. Perhaps at the beach I'll see real, live nudes. That could be interesting.

The price is right, about $30. I decide to sign up.

Al calls and reserves a spot for his bicycle tour and my scenic drive and beach tour. And then it's beddy-bye time.

Nov. 4 - Another Day at Sea

My shore excursion went to Kakao Beach on Orient Bay. Unfortunately, the beach was so crowded there were no lounges or beach umbrellas available for any of us on the tour.

NOV. 5 - OUR SINT MAARTEN SHORE EXCURSIONS

This morning, our ship docks at Philipsburg, the capital of Sint Maarten.

After breakfast in the Garden Cafe, we go ashore and wander through some of the port shops. They all seem to carry the same items: T-shirts, baseball caps, various types of resort wear, coffee mugs, shot glasses, sunglasses, jewelry and other touristy trinkets. I'm not much of a shopper. Don't like hauling stuff around as we travel. Most of our souvenirs are the photos we take.

But we wander for about an hour. Back at the ship, we are surprised to see an even larger ship parked next to ours. The Oasis of the Seas. This largest of all cruise ships dwarfs the Epic.

AL AND THE OASIS OF THE SEA

By the time I arrived in Sint Maarten, I'd gotten comfortable—more or less—with the sheer size of the Epic. You know: 50 percent more displacement than a nuclear-powered aircraft carrier. Epic, indeed.

Looking at our ship tied to the dock—or was the dock tied to our ship?—I was reminded of what they called the Boeing 747 when it first flew: "The Aluminum Overcast." Same concept here. We're talking big ship, folks. Seriously big. Whoa Mama size. Something that large actually floats?

Dutifully awed, I wandered off the quay with Sunny for adventures ashore. In our absence, another cruise ship, the Oasis of the Seas, arrived and tied up beside the Epic.

When we returned from our shopping venture, I simply could not believe what I was seeing. Looking up at the Oasis, I felt like a little kid standing on the sidewalk outside a skyscraper, looking skyward, mouth wide open.

In an instant, the Epic, big as she was, became ... well ... less epic. A saga reduced to a narrative. A 250-pound running back flattened by a 330-pound tight end. Definitely Whoa Mama size.

Back on board, I stepped out on the deck, facing the Oasis. All I could see in every direction, were balconies. Up, down, left, right, balconies. Scores and scores. How many cabins were there on that behemoth?

I put a wide-angle lens on my camera. Not wide enough. I took multiple shots for later compilation as a poster.

I think it's time to hit the soft ice cream machine. Chocolate with syrup and sprinkles. Mebbe a cookie. Big enough for me.

BEST OF SINT MAARTEN SCENIC DRIVE & BEACH

I head for the dock at 10:15 a.m. for my 11 a.m. tour, and realize that hundreds of us are going on this tour. We aren't all going in one bus, but we'll be flooding the beach at Orient Bay.

Obviously, we're all eager to float in the clean warm waters of Orient Bay or blissfully stretch out on a beach lounge and enjoy the sound and smell of the Caribbean.

I'm wearing my bathing suit under my slacks and tank top. I'm also wearing a sun hat and carrying my cruise ship tote. In the tote I have a beach towel provided by Norwegian, my digital camera, a note pad and pen, and a case for my sunglasses. I'm carrying a little cash so I can rent a beach lounge and umbrella, and buy a cool drink if I want. I feel well prepared for the tour.

As I've mentioned, this 37-square-mile island is shared by two different nations. Part of the island is an independent country within the Kingdom of the Netherlands; the other part is governed by the Republic of France.

The Dutch side became an independent nation Oct. 10, 2010. For numerology buffs, that's 10-10-10.

During our bus tour, the guide informs us that prices for gas and groceries on the Dutch side are listed in guilders. On the French side, in dollars.

The electrical outlets and electrical currents differ from one side to the other. Hotels on the Dutch side have outlets for 110 volts, 60 cycles. On the French side, hotel outlets will be for 220 volts, 60 cycles.

A Dutch-side hotel room TV will carry all the American networks and cable stations. The French-side TV, on the other hand, carries only French stations.

As our bus chugs through Philipsburg and other towns, and the on-board guide explains about the island and the famous people who come to Sint Maarten to enjoy the beaches, sadness fills me. Although the guide's narration is enthusiastic, all I see as I look out the window is poverty.

While the guide points out a hilltop mansion that belongs to Mick Jagger of the Rolling Stones, I glance down side streets and alleys lined with scrap metal houses and markets that resemble sheds.

Scrawny dogs nose through little piles of trash. My heart feels like a sweet scoop of ice cream melting into an icky, sticky puddle that attracts dust and flies.

After a while, I can't bear to look out the window anymore. Such striking contrasts: here I am on a lovely cruise, enjoying gourmet meals and great entertainment, and I'm riding through a town filled with the ashen bones of poverty. I remind myself that we cruise ship people provide employment for the locals, but the thought isn't very comforting.

All I want to do is swim in Orient Bay. Just swim in the gorgeous water, and let the beauty of the sky and sea and sand fill me.

When our bus reaches Kakao Beach, our guide says we have an hour and a half. He points out where the bus will be parked. "You must be back by 1:30," he says. "We cannot wait, so keep an eye on your watch."

We lumber off the bus, a string of older folks in hats hauling beach towels and tote bags. Between the bus, in its muddy parking spot, and the beach we've all come to enjoy, is a long, low row of bright green palm trees.

As I enter the shade of this palm tree forest, I see that this stand of trees shelters several welcoming bars and small cafes. The afternoon breeze drifts through, promising beauty and pleasure as waves slosh ashore in a lazy crazy rhythm, making me eager to go jump in. Emerging from the line of trees, I step into the hot white sand stretching between me and the sparkling blue of the bay.

The sandy beach is crammed with lounges. Row after row of white plastic lounges with pale blue padding, packed so closely together that you have to climb onto your lounge from the foot, rather than sitting down from the side. Large, deep blue umbrellas shade most lounges.

Almost all the lounges hold bathers. Bathers napping. Bathers drinking beer. Bathers drying off.

Beyond the beach full of loungers, scores of people are swimming or standing chest-deep in the sun-sprinkled bay.

"Where can I get a lounge?" I ask a waiter walking by with a tray of exotic drinks. He points to a counter not far from me.

Two well-tanned young men greet me with big smiles as I approach the counter. "I'd like a lounge and an umbrella, please," I say.

Their smiles fade. "All gone," one says.

"Excuse me?" I don't quite understand. "I can't get a lounge and umbrella here?"

"They're all taken." The other fellow sweeps his arm from one end of the beach to the other, showing me that every last lounge and umbrella is already occupied or claimed by others.

"But our tour bus just arrived. There will be many people like me here soon, wanting a lounge and umbrella," I say.

"Bad planning," one of the guys behind the counter says. "Too many people today."

"Now what do I do?" I wonder. The "scenic tour" was deeply disturbing. And now at the beach, I can't get a lounge to put my stuff on so I can go swimming.

An older couple from the bus is standing nearby. They, too, want a lounge and an umbrella. The three of us look at each other and then back at the guys behind the counter.

"So," I say. "What can we do? We want to go swimming."

"Oh, no problem," one of the young men responds. "Just walk along until you find an empty space, and lay your towel down."

I glance at the older couple. The man is rolling his eyes.

Well, I came here for one reason only and that's to swim. And I'm going to swim. "Okay." I turn and walk down a narrow path through the rows of blue lounges until I get to the water's edge, and then turn and head along the beach.

To my left is the bay. To my right is the long, long line of lounges and umbrellas. It's not easy walking through scorching soft sand. With each step, I sink and my sandals fill. So I take a moment to remove my sandals, shake the sand from them and put them in my tote. Then I continue trudging along the hot sand beach. Now my feet are really burning!

The older couple follows me. I don't know where I'm going, but I'm looking for some kind of break in the line of lounges. Some kind of sandy open space for my beach towel.

Eventually, I reach the end of the rows of lounges. And there I find an open space. I glance at the older couple and say, "I guess we just spread out our towels and put our clothes and stuff on them."

As I slip out of my slacks, I hear a woman's voice say, "This is our umbrella."

Looking up, I see three couples who have moved their lounges into a kind of circle so they can easily converse. The women hold tall drinks. The men are stretched out, everyone getting some sun. They all look healthy and wealthy and in their 30s or early 40s. It appears as though they're from a nearby resort hotel. A stone path leads from their lounges away from the waves and into a hotel garden near the palm tree forest.

On my side of the group an umbrella spreads a circle of shade on the hot afternoon sand, but no one is actually sitting under its shade. "That's our umbrella," one of the women repeats, her hard eyes glaring at me over her sunglasses.

"I know how precious they are," I say. "I tried to get a lounge and umbrella and they were all out. So I'm just going to put my stuff here." That's when I notice that a small portion of the umbrella's shadow is falling across my towel.

"I'm here to swim," I say, trying to explain that I don't want to crowd under their umbrella.

She's still glaring at me as if I'm a thief, an intruder encroaching on her territory.

"What do you want me to do?" I ask, stunned by her angry face and her attitude of ownership.

She rolls her eyes and glances at one of the men. I assume he's her husband.

"Are you asking me to move my towel farther away from your umbrella?" I ask, as I actually pull the towel out of the shade. "No problem," I say. I tug my towel farther away from the umbrella's shade.

The older couple who were following me do not move their towel. Part of it lies in the umbrella's shade. They're putting their hats and sandals on their towel, and the man is preparing to go in the water.

The next thing I know, the angry woman's husband comes over and closes the umbrella.

And they move their lounges so that their backs are to me, the older couple, and the closed umbrella.

I can't believe what's just happened. Talk about obnoxious. Talk about rude. And I know these people are from the states. They speak clear, unaccented American English. Their behavior is shameful. No wonder Americans have a bad reputation abroad.

As quickly as rage floods me, another truth fills me. When I was a kid, my parents took us on many travels. We didn't have a lot of money, but my mom and dad were full of creativity and a sense of adventure.

They took us to Yellowstone and to the Great Smoky Mountains. We went to Niagara Falls, Mammoth Cave and even spent a day at author Laura Ingalls Wilder's home in Mansfield, Missouri. On all our trips, we camped, pitching an old army tent and roasting marshmallows under starry skies.

Everywhere we went, my parents made friends. They'd invite the kids from neighboring campsites to come share our marshmallow roast. They'd share morning coffee with anyone who wandered by our tent.

Some of those traveling friendships lasted for decades.

I imagine how my mother would have reacted if she'd been among the group who "owned" the umbrella. To someone searching for a place to spread out their towel, she would have said, "Put your things under our umbrella. We'll keep an eye on them while you go swimming."

That's the joyous, generous spirit I grew up with. And as I stare at the backs of the arrogant group, I feel both anger against them and embarrassment for them. What shriveled, unhappy lives they're leading.

But I'm determined to enjoy the afternoon. So I fold my slacks and tank top and place them, along with my watch, glasses, hat and tote, on my towel.

The older woman is sitting on her towel, watching her husband as he heads for the water. "Would you mind watching my stuff?" I ask her. "I'll go swim for a while, then I'll come and return the favor so you can swim and not worry about your things."

She gives me a thumbs up, pulls a book out of her tote, and says, "Swim as long as you like."

The water is warm and welcoming I walk right in up to my neck, and then my feet leave the earth and I'm swimming. There is nothing to equal being swept away in the clear, blue waters of Orient Bay.

Although lots of people are enjoying the water and others floating above under parachutes pulled by motor boats, the bay is so vast I feel alone with the sea and the sky. And I'm as happy as one of the gulls wheeling overhead. The day is beautiful and I'm swimming free in the sparkling warm waters of the Caribbean.

All I feel is joy. The water buoys me. The sky above is endless blue as I paddle out and back, out and back. Then I lie on my back and simply float. The bay swells rise and fall gently, as if the ocean is breathing, lifting and lowering me, holding me in its loving embrace.

I swim and float and swim until I'm tired. When I walk back to my towel, the older woman joins her husband in the water.

The pleasure of water, sky and beautiful weather fills me with bliss. Even though the obnoxious people are still sitting around with their tightly closed umbrella, I'm happy that I've been able to do exactly what I wanted—swim in the clear, warm waters of the Caribbean.

Our hour and a half at Kakao Beach passes quickly, and soon we're back on the bus. Before we pull out, our guide counts every seat and discovers that two passengers are missing. He and the driver wait for five minutes. Then he takes off, running to see if he can find the missing passengers at a bar or on the beach. When he returns to the bus (no passengers in tow), he waits five more minutes.

"We can't wait any longer," he says, apologetically, "We must stay on schedule and we're already way too late."

With that, the bus driver pulls out. I wonder where the missing passengers are. And I wonder when they'll discover that the bus left them behind.

During the ride back to the ship, I share my seat with a woman from Staten Island, New York. As we talk about the cruise, sharing opinions, she tells me how much she loves the hypnotist Nadeen.

"I loved her show so much I saw it three times," she says.

I keep my thoughts about Nadeen's show to myself, and simply listen.

"I used to suffer terrible anxiety attacks," the woman continues, "but I learned some relaxation techniques, very much like the suggestions Nadeen gives during her show, and was able to free myself from the attacks."

The woman had attended a private or small-group event held onboard by Nadeen and her respect for the hypnotist had grown even more.

Our conversation reminds me that we all see things differently. Each person's opinion is unique, based on our individual experiences and our interpretation of those experiences.

***

Back in our room, I shower and wash my hair. Then I stretch out on our comfortable bed and write about the day in my notebook.

Al stumbles in shortly after 5:30 p.m., looking like he's about to collapse. Or as if he's in the process of collapsing. His lovely silver hair is desperately askew, his face sunburned, his entire body stooped and sagging, his eyes strained and desperate. As soon as he gulps down a pain pill, he sort of folds up onto the padded stool at the end of the bed and begins his tale of woe.

AL'S BICYCLE SHORE EXCURSION

I love my bicycle. It's a $50 Craigslist special with only three of 21 gears working, which makes it less tempting to thieves.

That said, it does a fine job carrying me hither and yon, though it and I are occasionally bypassed by older women in wheelchairs. When you have bad knees, as I do, speed doesn't count: just getting there does.

Thus, when I saw "Historical Philipsburg by Bicycle" as a Sint Maarten tour, I was smitten. Just the ticket: fresh air, a leisurely ride through points of interest, a "cold drink while chatting." Yes, there was a "climb"—two, in fact—but I can easily do a "short incline." Short. "Stop and rest point" looked equally appealing. Resting is high on my list.

A review of the tour's classifications showed that the bicycle tour was "family recommended." Also good news. It was, however, a Difficulty Level Two.

Difficulty Two involves a "considerable amount of physical activity such as uneven or steep terrain." It was not recommended "for guests with physical limitations."

I asked myself, "How difficult could a family activity be, which involved a pleasant bicycle ride along a beautiful bay?"

And so I signed on.

I will admit to some trepidation when our tour assembled. The guides—two of like mold—were young men in Spandex, clearly in training for the U.S. Olympic team. Broad of shoulder, narrow of waist, they were the very picture of healthy outdoor activity. As I once was. Once.

I was, however, comforted by the fact that several in our tour group were of mature years, as well as several others whose physical shape could best be described as "spherical." If they can do it, so can I, I thought. Chin up, tallyho, out of the trenches and charge.

In due course, we marched to our bicycles. These

were hybrid bicycles, sort of mountain-bike-ish but with skinny tires. We all made adjustments and rode around the car park, getting the feel for our bikes. A hybrid bike is flighty, taking a steady hand and a superb sense of balance.

I quickly realize that the island of Sint Maarten is not bicycle-friendly (serious understatement.) This is because there are few roads. Only one, to be specific, and it is packed with both cars and trucks.

We were, however, assured by our guides that the drivers were friendly and courteous: they only honk to say "hello." Sounded good to me.

And thus, our group of 22 rode toward the center of Philipsburg, sandwiched between curbs and tailpipes, keeping our flighty bikes carefully balanced while enjoying the fresh air of Sint Maarten—air that had just passed through a diesel lorry. It was truly exciting.

In due course, we crossed a footbridge and entered the Philipsburg boardwalk, better known as Margaritaville, stopping for some history of the island.

This is what I'd come for! I could have stayed all afternoon, and I daresay I wasn't alone in that regard.

But duty called, and so off we went down an alley into what we were told was "residential" Sint

Maarten. There we rode two abreast, blocking traffic, a much safer way to ride.

A bit of major traffic and we arrived at the foot of Little Bay Hill. It rose like the first incline of a roller coaster and was crowned with a two-lane road packed with cars.

One of my fellow bicyclists, a wiry middle aged German woman, softly uttered, "Grüss Gott."

We were told by our guides not to worry: Little Bay Hill is only an 18-percent grade. Eighteen percent? Stiff upper lip, old chap: you can do it.

This was where the sheep were sorted from the goats. The goats, far nimbler, downshifted their bikes to the lowest gear and endeavored to pedal their way to glory, or the rest stop, whichever came first.

We of more sheepish lineage dismounted and wheeled our rides up the sidewalk, afoot.

Again, in due course (I know I'm repeating myself), we arrived at the Look Out Point. The goats, having arrived long ago, were walking about looking fit. We who arrived later guzzled water and congratulated each other.

The view was indeed spectacular. "That's our ship? That little white thing on the horizon?" And so it was. More self-congratulation ensued.

As is often said on TV, "But wait, there's more."

We were only halfway up.

And so, to make a long story shorter, we flogged ourselves up another pitch and down a breathtaking grade into Divi Little Bay Resort.

It was here that we encountered our "second short incline." Even the goats gave up on this one.

The final pitch was, in fact, even too steep for bicycles, leaving us all to crawl up the last two blocks of the rocky slope. There, at the top, we arrived at Fort Amsterdam, built in 1631.

Those who could still stand were given a detailed and quite interesting history lesson. Pictures were taken (distant ships bobbing in the bay, old cannons, testimonial selfies). More water was guzzled. And we all felt pretty proud of ourselves.

Then realization set in. We have to go back. The way we came. And the ship sails in just over an hour. Where is the air-conditioned bus?

Suffice it only to say that I barely crawled up the gangplank onto the Epic at 5:25 p.m., five minutes before the departure deadline. The last I saw of my cyclemates, they were guzzling—margaritas, one assumes—in Philipsburg. I can only hope they sailed with the ship.

As I clung to the gangplank's rail, thinking only of a long shower and a handful of pain medication, a cheery woman approached and joyfully asked if I was a member of the bicycle tour. I think I replied, but I may have only nodded. There was nothing more to say.

***

We order room service: a fruit plate, turkey sandwich and chocolate cake with mixed berry compote.

Al takes a long, hot shower, then we both stretch out on the bed in our complimentary robes. He reads his Kindle. I write.

Al takes more pain medication before we turn off the light at 9 p.m., grateful for our quiet room and comfortable bed.

This block-long display greeted us as we wandered through downtown St. Thomas.

NOV. 6 - ST. THOMAS

Yesterday was Sint Maarten. Today we visit St. Thomas, our last port of call before we reach Miami.

Because St. Thomas, being part of the U.S. Virgin Islands, is our first port of call in the U.S., we're required to go through immigration. We'd received in our stateroom an immigration form to fill out, listing our names, home address, and other personal information.

The procedure this morning is swift. The immigration officer takes our form, looks it over, then checks our passports. And that's it. We're free to leave the ship and look around.

We find a cafe with affordable Wi-Fi: $10 for an hour. Al emails all our contacts, telling them we're back on U.S. soil, and still enjoying the trip.

I enjoy an iced latte and think about this transatlantic cruise. It certainly has not been boring.

After my beach fiasco and Al's bicycle-tour debacle, I suspect we're done with the island of Sint Maarten.

Only three more days, counting today, and our journey will be over.

In all, we will have spent 10 complete days at sea with nothing but ocean surrounding us. Miles of water, nothing but water. Water and sky. You might think that so many sea days would be wearying, but they haven't been.

The vibrant sea is always changing. It's pewter gray or it's deep blue or it's green or it's full of snowcapped waves. Overhead clouds change the color of the water or the angle of the sun's light.

Sunrises and sunsets are among the most beautiful experiences on a cruise. And the night sky. Well, what can I say?

There's something other-worldly about the night sky as seen from the middle of the ocean. Standing on deck under an immense blackness so deep it seeps into every wrinkled crevasse of your soul calms restlessness and worry.

Then there are the stars. Thousands, millions of them. Tiny points of light so bright they pierce the heart. Their abundance fills me with awe.

While night at sea feels reassuring, sunrise on a cruise is especially dramatic. Every morning is like the first morning ... nothing but sea and sky, and then the light, the thin line of white gold delineating sea from sky. The brilliance increases until a curve appears rising from the waters. The curve continues to rise, becoming a brilliant ball whose light streams across the waves in a radiant path.

I've seen more bright sunrises than dark skies on this cruise, mainly because we usually go to sleep early. Fourteen days of such beauty can enrich, perhaps even change, a person. Existing within such beauty for days on end certainly has an impact.

These thoughts and feelings fill me as we sit in the cafe.

Once Al finishes sending emails, we amble aimlessly among the many small shops crowding the harbor front. The fragrance of fresh fudge pulls us into one candy shop, and we end up with a little bag of sweets to nibble as we walk.

As noon approaches, we return to the ship and the Garden Cafe for a light lunch.

On board, we pause at one of the self-service (interactive) screens to reserve two seats for tonight's

9:30 show in the Epic Theater: "Legends in Concert." We've heard the show is good and, according to the screen, we got the last two seats in the house. We'll be there early to claim our chairs.

After lunch, we go back ashore and indulge in a long, lazy walk through town. Flags wave in the afternoon breeze, and sidewalk salesmen urge us to buy time-share condos.

I find the heat oppressive and Al doesn't like the humidity, but we're curious and so we continue to wander. We check out shops and cafes. We stop in a beautiful open-to-the-harbor bar and share iced lemonade while overhead fans that look like they're from a 1940s movie set cool us.

We explore a store specializing in embroidery and are amazed at the gorgeous tablecloths, place mats, pillow cases and other products on display.

When the heat and humidity wear us out, we return to the ship. And enjoy an afternoon nap in our air conditioned cabin.

***

At dinner, Al's back begins to hurt so much that he returns to our room for a pain pill. We both suspect this is a response to yesterday's bike ride.

By 9:30 p.m. the pill is working and he feels good enough to go to the Legends show with me.

We get good seats and settle in, ready to be entertained. The evening's three performers do their best to look and sound like Jimmy Buffet, Adele and Aretha Franklin. But the show turns out to be a disappointment.

If we were doing a thumbs up/thumbs down rating for the shows we've seen on board, this Legends concert would be a definite thumbs down. Right beside the hypnotist's performance.

While the singers are talented and work hard to present an entertaining evening, the ship's band is so unrelentingly loud we can't hear the lyrics let alone our own thoughts.

And the two women vocalists do as much screaming as singing—a total turn-off. Al and I wonder if our ear drums will be damaged by the excruciatingly loud music and by the equally excruciating screaming of "Adele" and "Aretha."

In addition, a sexist thread runs through all the sets. Tasteless jokes about men and women, marriage and romantic relationships. The audience does not respond well to the jokes, but the lack of laughter fails to curb the tasteless chatter between songs.

We are pleased when the concert ends and we can return to our room and climb into bed.

The evening view from our dinner table.

NOV. 7 - PASSENGER TALENT SHOW

We sleep so deeply that we don't wake up until after 8 a.m. Al immediately begins talking about last night's rotten show.

"Instead of calling it Legends, they should bill it as two loud women and somebody else," he says.

As we dress for breakfast I complain about the obnoxious marriage jokes.

"I think it's a generational thing," Al says. "By the time you're our age, if you're married, you know how precious your mate is. In your 20s and 30s you might identify with marital fighting and disappointment, sarcasm and drama. But by your 60s, you know how lucky you are to have a loving partner and a good marriage."

Heading for the Garden Cafe, I say, "I think part of my disappointment in the sexist humor comes from believing that we as a society had moved beyond all that rot. I thought we'd buried all that back in the '70s. And it shocked and dismayed me to see 'stars' on stage using it as part of their shtick, as part of their attempt to connect with an audience."

But as soon as we step into the Garden Cafe, all complaints cease and we're focused on breakfast. We enjoy fruit, croissants, French toast and cereal at a window table, with the sun dancing on the waves beside us.

Checking our *Freestyle Daily*, we see that in the Atrium at 10 a.m. there's a lecture on Norwegian ships and destinations.

At 10:30 there's a presentation called "Running a Floating Hotel" featuring the ship's hotel director, food and beverage director and the executive chef. Since I've already talked with the hotel director and executive chef, I'll pass on this event.

The rest of the day will be filled with games and performances.

Al decides to read his Kindle on the outside deck near the swimming pools, while I attend the lecture on Norwegian ships and destinations.

At the lecture (which is informative, but also resembles an hour long commercial) I learn that we are on the last transatlantic cruise for 2014. For the rest of this year and into next year, the Epic will cruise the Caribbean.

I learn that there are 14 freestyle cruising ships in the Norwegian fleet. I learn about the Norwegian ships that sail around the Islands of Hawaii, and those that cruise South America or Canada.

Even onboard "commercials" have interesting information and I enjoy the lecture.

THE BIG BINGO WIN

One of the most popular and ubiquitous cruise ship games is the familiar standby: Bingo.

On past cruises I've played a few cards of Bingo, but I've never won anything, so I don't bother anymore.

At lunch today in the Garden Cafe, Al and I hear a hilarious Bingo story. And it happened here on the Epic, during this transatlantic cruise.

As we settle down with our lunch trays, we overhear a lively discussion at the table next to us. Several women are talking about their adventures (or misadventures) in the casino.

These are middle-aged women, with short curls and soft curves. Grandmotherly women. Perhaps they're sisters or cousins or people who used to work together. It's clear they know each other well, and their various tales are relished fully. Each story results in a burst of laughter.

Luckily, we get to listen in on one tale from beginning to end. The woman telling it, I'll call her Sally, starts out by saying how much she loves Bingo. How she'd rather play Bingo than a slot machine because she thinks she's more talented than a slot machine. Everyone giggles at her words.

Then she talks about being a member of Alcoholics Anonymous and how meaningful that membership is to her. How glad she is that there are AA meetings on board. The way the other women respond, with teasing and understanding, I wonder if they're all part of AA.

"Well, you all know about my big win at the start of this cruise," she says.

"Yes, yes," one woman says. "What was the prize? $50?"

"Five hundred dollars." Sally raises on eyebrow and grins. "And one free game card for each Bingo game played on board for the rest of this cruise."

"Sally, you're the Bingo queen," one of the women says. Others join in with good humor, teasingly suggesting that Sally buy everyone dinner out of her Bingo winnings.

Another woman waves her hand for them to stop the teasing. "If you think that's a haul, wait 'til you hear what she won this morning," she says. Everyone grows quiet.

Sally says, "This morning I hit the jackpot on one of my free games. I actually hit the biggest prize of all."

"How much?" several women ask.

"Four thousand dollars."

The women whoop and cheer and reach across to give Sally some high fives.

Sally shakes her head and holds up her hand. "Wait," she says, "there's more to the story."

She continues, her smile not so bright. "When I went to collect my winnings, they told me that not enough people had played Bingo to actually raise the $4,000 kitty. So they don't have the money to give me."

Her friends begin to chuckle, eyes sliding sideways, connecting in disbelief and wicked delight.

"So," Sally says slyly, "to make up for not getting $4,000, they've given me a bottle of champagne."

The women burst into laughter, shrieking and pounding the table, convulsing in full-guffaw mode.

Al and I are laughing with them. An AA member who purportedly wins $4,000 can't collect her winnings because they don't really exist. Instead, she's given a bottle of champagne.

***

Our day rushes by and suddenly, it's 3 p.m., time for the Guest Talent Show in the Epic Theater. Cruise Director Armen Petrossian urged me to attend, so here I am in the 681-seat theater, wondering what I will see and hear.

My first surprise: Every seat is filled. Who would have guessed that a passenger talent show would be so popular with fellow passengers?

The MC welcomes us and introduces the first act: Jim from Hawaii playing the ukulele and singing. Jim walks out on stage with his ukulele.

He says he's 67 and has been playing the uke for only two years. He invites us to sing along with him. Then he plays and sings "Somewhere Over the Rainbow." And the entire theater sings with him. We sound quite lovely.

Next is hospital engineer Steven from Ireland. He sings "Danny Boy" in a beautiful and plaintive voice.

Then another ukulele player, this one from Kansas.

The comedy team "Ray and Richard" from New York are fairly funny. One is a retired electrical engineer, the other a retired tax collector. Their act reminds me of the kind of thing my uncles used to do for family gatherings. A mixture of one liners and cute stories.

There are performers from Germany and England, from Florida and Boston and Kansas. Some are better than others, but the audience loves them all. Isn't it amazing that on this mega-ship filled with 4,000 passengers, there's a real sense of community right here, right now. It feels like a family get together—and that feels good.

A man named Larry is the talent show closer. He describes himself as an American gainfully unemployed in Ecuador.

Dressed in a black tux, red tie, red cummerbund and black hat, he is elegance personified. Slim and with a full mane of white hair, he moves gracefully to the music as he sings "Night and Day."

It's like watching Frank Sinatra or Fred Astaire or some similar performer who just loves to perform for an audience. It's all beautiful—the music, his well-choreographed moves, the audience's enthusiasm.

Larry is a true showman.

And when he ends his act by tossing his hat into the audience, the audience goes wild with cheers and applause.

***

Al and I enjoy a leisurely and satisfying dinner in the Manhattan Dining Room. He has roast beef. I have chicken cordon bleu. And as we dine, we watch the sky beyond our window.

The evening view is always interesting. Usually clouds rise above our wake. Sometimes they're huge and fluffy white. Sometimes they have a golden glow.

Tonight, as sunlight begins to fade, the sky grows dark with knotted clouds, and way out on the horizon we can see a storm, black and violent. But close to the ship, the air is calm. A few minutes later, we're delighted by a fat rainbow stretching between the dark clouds and ocean on the horizon.

After dinner, up on Deck 15, we simply stroll. We have the outside deck all to ourselves as night's blackness gathers close until we feel we're held in its hands.

There are no stars tonight. The sky is full of clouds. We squeeze together in the chilly wind, arms tightly wound around each other, trying to stay warm. It's black and mysterious out here, with the wind messing up our hair.

Then the pitch-black clouds part slightly and a white disk of a full moon slides out.

"Wow," I say. "First a rainbow. Then a full moon."

As quickly as it appears, just that quickly it slips behind night's mantle and all is dark again.

How the Deck 15 pools, hot tubs and water slides look without all the passengers.

NOV. 8 – OUR LAST FULL DAY OF THE CRUISE

When we return from breakfast, we find an invitation in our mailbox. Here's what it says:

> As one of our special guests on board, we would like to invite you for the 'Premiere' of our new Cirque Dreams show. The show will be on the 8th of November, 2014, in the Spiegel Tent, Deck 6 Forward at 4:30 p.m. Doors open at 4 p.m.
>
> See you there!

The invitation is signed by Richard Janicki, hotel director.

How exciting is this! We get to see another Cirque Dreams show! A new and different Cirque Dreams show. A perfect way to spend our last evening at sea.

Late morning, the captain addresses us through the ship's PA system. "This is the old man on the bridge," he says. Then he talks about the weather, our location and when we will be docking at Miami.

He describes tomorrow's disembarkation and how to prepare, giving us all kinds of instructions.

We've bought a transfer pass so it should be easy for us. We'll leave, go through customs, and climb aboard a bus (transportation the cruise line has arranged) that will take us to the airport. And then, a not-so-long flight from Miami to San Francisco. Friends will meet us at SFO. We'll spend the night at their place. The next morning, we'll catch the bus home concluding our fabulous trip.

Lunch at Taste, with live piano music in the background.

This will be our last lunch onboard and we're not eager to end it. We linger over dessert.

Although we've eaten daily at three Epic restaurants—the Garden Cafe Buffet, the Manhattan Dining Room, and Taste—there are other complimentary dining venues on the ship. I call them "complimentary" because they are included in the price of the cruise. We could have had breakfast, lunch, dinner or late-night fare at O'Sheehan's Neighborhood Bar & Grill.

Located mid-ship on Deck 6, O'Sheehan's is like a neighborhood pub. It serves wings, nachos, fish & chips, chicken pot pie and other comfort foods. Breakfasts include omelets, French toast, egg platters with breakfast meats, and baked goods.

There's also the Spice H2O lunch buffet near the pools on Deck 15 where we've gotten a munch or two during this cruise. Sandwiches and salads.

And, of course, there is always room service.

For room service between midnight and 5 a.m., there's a charge. Otherwise, it comes with the cruise.

In addition to the restaurants included in the price of the cruise, Epic offers specialty restaurants that charge for their lunches and dinners.

Here's a list of the Epic's specialty restaurants:

Cagney's Steakhouse

La Cucina (Italian)

Le Bistro (French)

Moderno (Churrascaria, or Brazilian style steakhouse)

Shanghai (Asian)

Spiegel Tent (Circus/Dining)

Teppanyaki (Japanese)

Noodle Bar (Chinese)

Wasabi (Japanese)

Yakitori & Sushi (Japanese)

Lots of choices when it comes to mealtimes.

As with virtually every other day on our trip, today's weather is perfect. Bright and breezy. Not too warm. We wander the ship, glancing in shops, going outside to stand at the rail and watch the sea go by. On this gentle and lazy day for us, we savor the last few hours of our big trip.

AL'S EXPANDING HORIZONS

NOAA (the National Oceanic & Atmospheric Administration) tells us that 70 percent of the surface of the earth is covered with water.

This means that of the Earth's 197 million square miles of surface area, just under 140 million square miles are covered with water. This is one of those almost-meaningless statistics; well beyond the ability of the human mind to scale.

I'm a no stranger to oceans. I've been along the shores of both the Pacific and the Atlantic and have crossed both oceans by air. Yet, those experiences never gave me a real sense of the vastness of the ocean.

Coastal voyages go from port to port. Airplanes zip across in a matter of hours. Either way, the security of the shore is an ever-present comfort, even if just over the horizon. "Ocean? Yeah. No big deal."

In my office, I have a picture of a goldfish in a

small bowl, about to be emptied into a lake. The caption says, "Your horizons are about to expand." And so were mine, as we sailed with the Epic from Funchal to the Caribbean across the Atlantic.

It took the Epic seven days at sea to cover the 3,000 miles between those ports, a distance equal to the width of the continental United States. One week, steadily plowing along. No rest stops. Breakfast view: the ocean. Lunch view: the ocean. Supper view: the ocean. Day after day.

Twice, a ship appeared on the far horizon, passed, and disappeared behind us. That was it.

What made the ocean even more vast to me was traveling in a mega-ship. One hundred-fifty-thousand tons displacement. Six thousand passengers and crew. Nineteen decks. All that, and we were little more than a tiny speck on an endless span of blue. If humankind ever goes out to the stars, crossing interstellar space surely won't be much different than sailing the Atlantic on the Epic.

You might ask if I was bored. Never. There was much to do, books to read, sweets to eat. Beyond that, though, there was time to reflect; an opportunity to re-scale myself. I need to do that now and then.

It is my hope that, should you ever have opportunity

to take a long sea voyage such as the Epic's Atlantic crossing, you immediately sign up. Your horizons, like mine, will be expanded.

***

CIRQUE DREAMS

When the time arrives, we go to the Spiegel Tent to see the new Cirque Dreams show. We learn that 180 people have been invited to be guests of the ship at this performance, showcasing a new cast and new acts. Not everyone invited comes.

We are served complimentary drinks: alcoholic or soft drinks.

And when the show starts we are once again blown away with the athleticism, the grace, the strength and beauty of the performers.

One aspect of this new show is the strongman element. Two young men who are nothing but muscle perform a gymnastic act that includes handstands, head stands, aerial balancing and more. Their power and gracefulness are astonishing.

Another addition, a tight-rope walker, wows us as she prances on a not-so-tight rope above us.

The beautiful and amazing trapeze artists, the jugglers, the magical costume changes, the roller skaters—all are stunning.

The show is fantastic. What a wonderful ending to our cruise.

***

Actually, the perfect ending happens after the show.

We go to the Garden Cafe for supper around 8 p.m. The place is overflowing with passengers. People are eating, talking, visiting with friends they've met on board. They are hugging and kissing and promising to keep in touch.

As we walk with our trays (grilled salmon, grilled veggies and a generous scoop of paella), I see Magician Christian Miro eating alone at a small table. He wears a colorful bandanna on his head, but his thick dark curls peep out, giving him a cute, childlike appearance.

Once Al and I claim a two-person table, and place our plates and silverware on it, Al heads off to get us a beverage. And I walk to Christian's table.

"Excuse me," I say. When he looks up, I ask, "Are you Christian, the magician?"

His dark eyes dance above a mischievous smile. "It depends," he says. "If you liked my show, I am."

I gush about his show. I tell him I saw both the

noon-time close-up magic show and the full-blown evening performance. Then I tell him about my brother who has been a magician for years. I say I'm going to tell my brother about Christian's two wonderful illusions I'd never seen before.

Christian wants to know which tricks I'm referring to. I tell him that one was a very long trick based on a dream he had.

The other was a twist on a common card trick. The common trick is that the magician has an audience member sign a playing card, and put it in a deck. The magician shuffles the deck, tells a story or two, and at the end of the trick, the signed card is found inside the magician's wallet (which has been in his back pocket all along).

Christian Miro's twist on this trick had the entire deck of cards turning up in his pocket, and only the signed card remained in his hand.

He seems delighted with my enthusiasm for his performance.

I know the hours and hours of practice it takes to perform the illusions in a magic show. And his performances were fun and amazing.

I ask if he is related to the artist Joan Miro.

"We're some kind of distant relative," he says. "But

nothing close. I don't even know the relationship."

I tell him that Al and I visited the Joan Miro museum in Barcelona. "The museum was not as much fun as your shows," I say and he laughs.

Returning to our table, I'm happy that I had a few minutes to tell Christian Miro how much we enjoyed his magic. What a pleasant way to end our cruise.

***

Back in our room, we pack our bags for the last time. We empty the closet, not-so-carefully folding shirts and slacks. We keep out only what we'll wear tomorrow and our toothbrushes and tooth paste.

We'll carry our backpacks (keeping with us our precious documents, medications, cameras, notebooks and other things we need).

Everything else, we stuff into our suitcases. We attach the brown ID tags that we received this morning. Tomorrow, after we leave the ship, we'll find our bags in the "brown" section of the huge warehouse next door.

Tonight, once everything is packed away, we set our bags just outside our door, and retire.

How Miami looked to us at the end of our transatlantic cruise.

NOV. 9 - MIAMI

We're so eager for home that we wake up at 5:30 a.m. and again at 6:30 a.m., and finally get up at 7.

Our final bill is sitting in our mailbox. It's more than I expected, but the $88 haircut and the $27 laundry and the money we spent on shore excursions in Madeira and Sint Maarten along with other, smaller expenses, added up. Still, the cost is far less than what we would have paid for two airline tickets.

We share our last breakfast at the Garden Cafe. Looks like everyone else on board is having their last breakfast here, too. The place is buzzing. People making sure they say good bye to friends they met onboard. People exchanging email addresses, promising to stay in touch. People slipping bananas or apples into their totes to insure they'll have something to eat a little later this morning. (I guess after 14 days of constantly available food, it must feel sort of like "deprivation" to think you might have to actually wait for something to eat).

My omelet has no ham because the ship is out of ham. Al's oatmeal has no raisins because the ship is out of raisins. But we enjoy our breakfast croissants and the stunning views of Miami's skyline. All the skyscrapers shine in the morning sun, their reflections perfectly reproduced in the mirror-still water.

At 8:30 a.m. we head down to Deck 6 to disembark.

Our voyage has ended.

Our memories will last forever.

AL'S POST-CRUISE MUSINGS

(penned March 18, 2016)

When *Sunny announced she'd booked our return from Europe on Norwegian Cruise Line's Epic, I immediately went online to learn about the ship. The stats were impressive.*

But what did the reviews say?

That's when the Blue Bird of Happiness departed my feeder. There were lots of reviews, the majority critical. There were complaints about the cabins (small and strangely laid out), the food (average at best and without variety), and cigarette smoke drifting from the casino. A goodly number of complaints spoke of finding no place to escape from the herd.

But worst of all, there was no library. Transatlantic and no library? All those days at sea and nothing to read? What were they thinking? A feeling of dread began to fill me.

I'll confess that I made my wife's life somewhat

225

difficult in the weeks before departure. "What have you gotten us into, beloved-of-Al?" I was not a happy camper, and I let her know it. A husband's duty is to let his wife know when she's made a mistake, yes? (No.)

So now that the voyage is over, what are my thoughts? Do I owe an apology to my wife or an I-told-you-so? Should I take her out to dinner, or just lunch? Or should she take me? (The correct answer is always: Take her out. Dinner.)

Looking back at our cruise, I can say this: Our cabin was creatively designed. That's the word. Truth be told, I think the blueprints got caught in the copier when NCL started construction.

It's not that I mind using a restroom stall, but I'd rather that the walls were something more substantial than frosted glass. And there's something too intimate about brushing your teeth in the bedroom.

Overall cabin score: Thank goodness I'm 75 and a vet. We ex-military can sleep anywhere.

Since we inside-cabin voyagers only return to our cabin to sleep and change, how were the outside decks? I feared the worst. With so many people on board, would the ship be top-heavy when all that flesh headed for the pools on Deck 15?

To my delight, those fears proved groundless. On

the whole, we passengers got along well with each other. That granted, if sitting in the sun was your wish, it was essential to get there early to get a deck lounge. And once found, it was necessary to sit in it. No dropping-the-towel-and-leaving.

I really liked the interactive touch screens throughout the ship that enabled us to order tickets for various evening entertainments. They were efficient and required no standing in line (an important consideration for someone like me, with arthritic knees).

As to food, I was delighted to discover that earlier reports of troopship-quality fare were simply not true. And yes, I've eaten on a troopship.

The offerings in both the Epic's dining rooms and buffet were varied and tasty. I consider that an accomplishment of the first order, especially when considering the size of the ship's contingent and the long time we were at sea.

Best of all (at least to me) was the dessert selection. Would you believe pie? I can't remember seeing pie at sea before. And there was this wonderful chocolate pudding down in the Carlos' Bake Shop in the Atrium, the ideal mid-morning nosh.

If you believe, as I do, that sugar is a food group

at or near the core of the food pyramid, the Epic is your ship.

Besides the lack of a decent library, I was disappointed that there were no regularly scheduled religious services on board. We've cruised on other ships that offered both daily and Sunday worship services. But not the Epic.

So, the bottom line. Would I do it again? The answer is yes.

If you have the time, there's no better way to cross The Pond than by ship, and the Epic does a fine job. You may correctly read that as an endorsement (and I'm not being paid to say this, but I am open to a small gratuity).

Aside from this cruise and this ship, there is something about travel itself that needs to be acknowledged.

I didn't travel much as a kid. My kin were all stay-at-home types, with the exception of my father, a captain in the merchant marine who sailed with American President Lines.

I have one memory from when I was very young, of standing on the deck of his ship, probably tied up in San Francisco, utterly taken by the experience. Was that the seminal event in my lifelong wanderlust?

As soon as I said goodbye to Washington High School, I enlisted in the Navy. And in short order, found myself sitting in a Douglas DC-6B—that's a four-engine propeller airplane—on the runway at Travis Air Force Base in Vacaville, California, headed west across the Pacific.

And in what seemed an equally short time, I found myself on the foredeck of the U.S.S. General Mann, a WWII troopship, headed back east across the Pacific.

I'd seen a lot of the world, not all of it especially attractive. But the die was cast. It was a big world out there, and I wanted to go see it.

Fifty-plus years later, I can say I've seen it, and the itch to see more is still there. Last time I added it up, there were 32 countries and something like 46 states on my been-there list. More to come. Plans are afoot.

What have I learned?

I've learned that every place one goes there's always something interesting to learn. I've learned that people are usually helpful and kind, particularly so if you have five words in their language.

I've learned that every person and every place has a story, and it is those stories that make up the tapestry of humankind.

Perhaps I could have learned these things without

setting foot outside my hometown, but travel has given me a bigger picture, a larger view of the world. In this difficult age, I know that's important.

For me, the very thought of traveling, of going off to see something new, someplace different, is exciting.

When do we leave?

Where's my passport?

Are you coming?

SUNNY'S AFTERTHOUGHTS

Al was pretty sure he'd hate a mega-ship. But he didn't.

I had no preconceived ideas about mega-ships, but I was interested in what it would be like to cruise on one. And I've got to say, I loved it. I loved all the many choices. So many places to eat. So many different shows to take in.

And most people on a cruise are pretty happy, so it's fun getting acquainted with them and sharing stories.

Although there were an awful lot of passengers on board, the ship seemed crowded only in certain places (like near the swimming pools). Since I wasn't going to the most popular places most of the time, the crowds did not infringe on my enjoyment.

Many places aboard ship were totally abandoned much of the day—beautiful places with comfortable chairs and couches. Al and I claimed several as our own, where we played Scrabble on the iPad or we sat and read. So the idea that you'll find yourself constantly crushed amid throngs on a mega-ship ship is incorrect.

At the same time, I must add that we experienced crowds at the entertainment events and in the Garden Cafe. Not constantly, but now and then.

Looking back at our transatlantic cruise, I appreciated having so many long and lovely sea days. Just being in the middle of the ocean, gliding along with nothing but sea and sky, felt luxurious to me. That kind of beautiful, slow, quiet time encourages reflection and, to some extent, renewal.

I like to work, and when not on vacation, my days are usually chock-full of creative projects and other busy engagements.

The older I've grown, however, the more I've appreciated slowing down.

Taking an unhurried pace through the day can deepen and enrich insights. I realize that some people feel uncomfortable if they're not always busy. But disconnecting from the constant interruptions of Internet, telephone and TV can feel amazingly free. Such freedom, such unaccustomed openness, allows life in all its generous variety to flow in, filling us with a sense of newness we may not have experienced for decades.

Travel is challenging in all kinds of ways. You're out of what my mother called "the comfortable rut of your daily life." You're in unfamiliar surroundings, eating unfamiliar food, often unable to read the local papers or understand the local language. I find the newness of it all stimulating, even exciting.

The other day I saw a question on Facebook that asked: When was the last time you did something for the first time? And I thought, when we travel we're always doing something for the first time. Just about every day we're doing something we've never done before.

And all that newness is enriching. It stretches our lives, making them bigger and more interesting.

Because we have such great times when we travel, I encourage you to make your travel dreams come true. It may take some planning, some budgeting and a little courage, but the joy of making a dream come true will stay with you forever.

The nice thing is that you don't have to be rich or young or at the peak of health to enjoy a cruise such as this one. We are none of those things and we had the time of our lives on this trip. And we came home with plenty of memories and stories to tell.

Thank you for sharing our cruise across the Atlantic.

ACKNOWLEDGEMENTS

Although it can be true that writing is a lonely art practiced in isolation, this book is the result of many helpful people to whom we are indebted.

There are my inspiring writer friends who continue to encourage our efforts.

The group of friends I met in 2009 on the Scribd.com website: Barbara Alfaro, Laura Novak, Ingrid Ricks, Suzanne McLain Rosenwasser and Carla Sarett. Although our genres and writing styles differ, these accomplished authors have freely shared their knowledge and insight over the years, making the work of writing and indie publishing less lonely and worrisome. Their continuing friendship warms my heart.

Members of Writers Unlimited in Calaveras County, California, and members of the Redwood Writers Club in Sonoma County, California, have been an unending source of support and inspiration.

And there are others without whose help this book may never have come into being.

Celia H. Miles, an accomplished North Carolina author and editor, served as copy editor for this work, giving our work two careful readings and helping polish up our slightly-ragged manuscript.

Artist and designer extraordinaire, Parker Wallman, developed our cover design, capturing the wonder and beauty we experienced as our ship made its way across the great Atlantic.

We thank the many Epic staff members who devoted time and attention to us: from Cruise Director Armen Petrossian and Executive Chef Kevin Green to Hotel Director Richard Janicki. Louis from guest services and maître d' Violeta Bratu afforded us every courtesy, making us feel at home on our first Norwegian Cruise Line cruise.

And, as always, we must thank you, dear reader, for you are the reason we've written this book. Without you, we'd have little motivation to write about our travels.

AUTHOR REQUEST

If you have enjoyed our book, please tell your friends about it. We appreciate when our readers spread the word online and in person. It's a great encouragement to us.

And if you have the time and are so inclined, we welcome reader reviews and ratings. Leaving your opinion helps other readers know if our book is something they'd like.

Simply go to our book's page at Amazon.com to leave your comments and ratings. You can easily reach our book's page by typing the title and/or our byline into the Amazon.com search bar.

Thank you.

ABOUT THE AUTHORS

Al and Sunny Lockwood have traveled by foot, car, rail, air and cruise ship.

They've camped in national parks, hiked mountain trails, photographed springtime flowers in Death Valley and wintry surf along the rugged beaches of Northern California.

They've watched July 4th fireworks over Lake Tahoe, explored the Taos Pueblo, photographed the wild mustangs of Corolla, North Carolina, and ridden the Great Smoky Mountains Railroad through forests ablaze with autumn colors.

And everywhere they go, they capture unforgettable moments—Al with his camera and Sunny with her reporter's notebook. Their work has been published in magazines and newspapers. It has been recognized with awards from the National Federation of Press Women, the California Newspaper Publishers

Association, and the National Indie Excellence Awards.

This photograph was taken in an Athens coffee shop, when Al and Sunny ducked inside to escape a sudden downpour.

You can contact the Lockwoods at **sunnyandallockwood@gmail.com**, or like their facebook cruising page at **www.facebook.com/ cruisingpanamascanal?ref=hl**

TRAVEL MEMOIRS BY AL & SUNNY LOCKWOOD

What reviewers say about *Cruising Panama's Canal:*

"Their writing is inviting, funny, contagious and just flat out a joy to read."
> – William D. Curnutt (Amazon Vine Voice)

What readers say:

"Fascinating, funny, educational, romantic, sweet, insightful book. Al's ... mouth-watering descriptions of the desserts made me want to rip the pages out and eat them."
> – Karen Zaccheo

"Great book. Couldn't put it down."
> – R. Brockett

CRUISING THE MEDITERRANEAN

From the luminous canals of Amsterdam and Venice to the stunning mosaics of Istanbul's Blue Mosque, this travel memoir takes readers on the trip of a lifetime.

Al & Sunny Lockwood

What reviewers say about *Cruising the Mediterranean*:

"I think the Lockwoods could write about anything and make it interesting."
– Oak Tree Reviews

What readers say:

"The pictures are beautiful and the narrative pulls the reader right in."
– Avid Reader

"Just delightful!"
– Robert Johnston

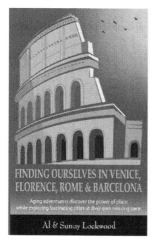

What readers say about ***Finding Ourselves in Venice, Florence, Rome & Barcelona***:

"What pleasurable reading! The beauty of these wonderful places shines through every page. I recommend this book for Baby Boomers and others whose hearts long to travel. You'll feel like you're right there ....

– Rick Bava, author of
In Search of the Baby Boom Generation

"I have thoroughly enjoyed living my dream through the words of Sunny and Sweetheart. Easy to read and fully descriptive, with travel tips well worth noting."

– C. Cherry

"What a delightful journey! ... With this book I joined Sunny and Al Lockwood on their journey to these beautiful sites and also visited Barcelona. I recommend this book for travelers ..."

– Diane Dreher, Ph.D.

Made in the USA
San Bernardino, CA
12 August 2020